ADVENTURES UNFORESEEN

Recollections of a PR Pioneer

Bryan Samain

All paper used in the printing of this book has been made from
wood grown in managed, sustainable forests.

ISBN 978-1-907938-75-7

Printed and published in the UK

Leiston Press
Unit 1b Masterlord Industrial Estate
Leiston
Suffolk
IP16 4JD

A catalogue record of this book is available from
the British Library

Cover design by Leiston Press

To Helen, Paul and Peter

Also by Bryan Samain:

Commando Men

Personal Encounters

The Author

Bryan Samain started his career in journalism. After service in World War II as a young Royal Marines Commando officer he returned to Fleet Street but soon decided to enter the comparatively new field of public relations – one of the first persons to do so in post-war Britain.

Over a period of thirty years he handled PR for some of the biggest companies in the country, including British Steel, Ford Motor Company and EMI. He now lives in retirement in Suffolk.

Contents

Year One: 1948

In 1948 the world of public relations was a world largely unknown to me, as it was to many others. Even though on my return to Fleet Street journalism from war service I had come into contact with a few PR people from time to time, I knew very little about them – what they did or what they were supposed to do.

But PR in Britain was beginning to catch on as a business activity. It meant different things to different people, of course, (it still does) but it soon became clear to me that conduct was the heart of it. Good conduct and good performance merited good publicity, the reverse entailed 'trying to show things in the best possible light' usually. Technically speaking, the effective handling of editorial publicity in written, spoken and visual terms was the best way to reach any audience convincingly.

For journalists generally, and especially those returning from the war, jobs were often hard to come by. It was difficult to get hired by newspapers, or magazines for that matter, on account of newsprint and paper rationing. Daily newspapers had no more than four pages to fill, and magazines were proportionally limited in terms of the amount of paper they had licences for. So quite a number of journalists, and I was one of them, began to look at PR as a means of employment, and to consider 'crossing the line' from press to public relations work, either with one of the independent PR consultancy firms beginning to spring up or with the in-house PR and publicity departments of major industrial companies.

I started with Alan Campbell-Johnson, at that time one of the few PR experts in Britain. He had just returned from

India where he had been serving as press relations advisor to Earl Mountbatten, the last viceroy, charged with handing back power to the Indians after 200 years of British rule. He was setting up a consultancy in London with Athena Crosse, a highly experienced journalist who had worked for many years principally with *Vogue*.

My work for Alan was to help launch a magazine for Esso UK, the oil company, one of his biggest clients. The magazine was aimed at important business contacts and customers, and was designed to show the company at its best. I spent much of my time working in close collaboration with Hans Wild, a former photographer for *Life*, the famous American news-picture magazine.

Hans was an American who spoke with an impeccable Oxford accent. He had worked in London for several years before starting a successful industrial and fashion photographic agency, acquiring the necessary finance to do so by deliberately getting himself fired from *Life* and securing a year's pay in compensation. Whilst working for *Life* he produced a notable photo-essay on the Bank of England, being the first photographer ever allowed inside the bank's bullion vaults to take pictures.

Hans and I toured the UK together, visiting various Esso locations to gather material for industrial features for the new magazine. The work was rather dull after Fleet Street journalism, and it was not enlivened by the committee that Esso established to 'vet' every word of copy before publication. The committee meetings took longer (far longer in some instances) than it took to write the features being scrutinized, and I found it all rather trying.

On the lighter side, one of Campbell-Johnson's other clients was the Jantzen swimsuit company. All they required was to have a picture of a smiling girl in a Jantzen bathing costume published in the *Sunday Pictorial* every week free of charge, giving them excellent product publicity. We (and the *Pictorial*) used to oblige accordingly, taking two or three girl models down to the south coast every Tuesday, irrespective of the weather, and photograph them in various poses – on the beach or in the waves – for the newspaper's issue the following Sunday. The models were brave and hardy girls; it was usually bitterly cold when they had to strip off. They also went to considerable trouble to enhance the look of their breasts by strapping them up with sticking plaster whenever the need arose.

Aside from my somewhat hesitant entry into the world of PR, my first book was published in 1948. It was a book about my wartime experiences entitled *Commando Men*. It sold quite well in the UK, but even better in the Commonwealth. I did not realise it then, but this book was going to be around for much of the rest of my life. It was re-published by three separate publishing houses, in hardback and paperback, in 1976, 1988, 2005 and 2014, one of the publishers going so far as to call it a minor classic of wartime reporting.

1950

Early in 1950 I met Howard Marshall. The meeting was to prove a turning point in my career.

'HM', as he was affectionately termed by all those who worked for him, had had a most distinguished life in journalism and radio broadcasting before entering the steel industry, which was where I came to know him. Aged 50 (he was the age of the century) and a handsome, well-built man, his eventful life had ranged from youthful sporting triumphs and service as a young RN midshipman in the First World War to sports writing, mainly cricket and rugby, for the *Daily Telegraph*. A former Oxford rugby blue who gained a trial cap for England in his youth, he became best known in the 1930s as a cricket commentator for the

BBC – the BBC's very first cricket commentator in fact. His informal and highly knowledgeable style when reporting test matches made him internationally famous. He also covered state occasions for the BBC, including two coronations, and broadcast on social issues such as slum housing, a radio report that alone brought in over 10,000 letters from listeners.

Howard Marshall was a very human person – a gentle giant who rarely lost his temper and who had an unwavering concern for human problems. Retiring from the BBC at the end of World War II, he was invited to undertake human relations and PR work for a newly formed steel company of which Sir Ernest Lever, a prominent City figure, had become chairman. Richard Thomas & Baldwins (RTB for short) was the product of a merger of two steel companies that had formerly been bitter commercial rivals. Marshall's primary task was to develop better internal relationships across the entire new organisation. To assist him, he gathered around him a mixed team of experienced specialists and talented young people.

The team included technical education and training experts, doctors (for steelworks medical centres), catering advisers, and several young professional communicators. Among the latter were Denis Thomas, who later became deputy editor of ITN and a respected art critic; Philip Nunan, a talented graphic designer and artist; Peter Hewitt, a young photo-journalist who became assistant editor of *Queen* magazine; and Mary Archard, my secretary, who broke into Fleet Street journalism and became a successful columnist on the *London Evening Standard.*

I was recruited by Howard Marshall initially to set up the editorial team and to develop company publications. Between us we produced employee newspapers and magazines, a company newsreel for screening in local steelworks cinemas, and shop floor 'briefing easels' to carry simplified economic information to steelworkers in the mills. It was all highly innovative at the time, and attracted a good deal of attention from other companies. My own work involved frequent travel around the country, usually with a photographer, getting material for use in our publications. RTB was a large company with over 40 works and 24,000 employees, so there was a good deal of territory to cover, mainly in South Wales, the Midlands and Lincolnshire.

I still retain firm memories of most of the works I used to visit. The vivid glare and heat and dust of Ebbw Vale is foremost. Sprawling along an entire valley for some three miles, its central feature was the first continuous hot strip mill to be built in Britain – and for that matter the first of its kind to be built outside the United States. It started production shortly before the outbreak of war in 1939, one of its first orders being for thousands of tons of corrugated steel sheet for Anderson air raid shelters to be erected in people's back gardens. Its basic product, however, was wide steel sheet for motor vehicles, turned out from the mile-long strip mill in enormous quantities – 600,000 tons a year. It was also a major supplier of steel sheet for makers of washing machines, refrigerators and other domestic products, as well as tinplate for boxes and canned goods.

In Lincolnshire there was Redbourn Works at Scunthorpe, one of the several iron and steelworks in the town owned by RTB and other companies. Scunthorpe was 'Steeltown' in the true sense of the word: the glow from its blast furnaces lit the skies at night, and the town's proud motto was 'The heavens reflect our labours'.

In the Midlands there were smaller works, most of them old-fashioned and well on the road to obsolescence. They had all been originally built and owned by Baldwins Ltd, the family steel firm that had merged with Richard Thomas

& Co in 1948 to form RTB. Stanley Baldwin had at one time been a director of the company. I remember visiting Wilden Works at Stourport-on-Severn and being shown the small room, with a large rolltop desk in one corner, that had once been Stanley Baldwin's office. There were elderly workmen there, too, who spoke of him with quiet pride and affection, remembering him as 'the gaffer' who used to walk round the works and talk to them to ask how they and their families were.

Across the Midlands, from Worcestershire to Northamptonshire, there was Irthlingborough iron ore mine, where tough teams of miners – most of them Polish in the 1950s – blasted and dug out tons of local ore for despatch by special weekly train to Ebbw Vale. The mine was entered by railcar down a large man-made cave, descending gradually to only a couple of hundred feet or so from ground level. Unlike coal mines, it was relatively easy to walk about on arrival, even at the mine face. There was plenty of height between the massive square pillars of stone supporting the roof that the miners left behind them as they worked forward.

As a sort of treat, the mine manager would invite visitors (including me) to 'press the plunger' in the charge box and detonate the dynamite drilled and placed in the wall for the next excavation. The resultant explosion would bring down heaps of dust and a shower of small stones, temporarily put the lights out, and (in my case) invariably push my miner's helmet over my eyes and reduce me to fits of laughter. All part of the day's work, of course...

1953

Still with Howard Marshall and enjoying every minute, I became involved in a strange PR affair early in 1953.

The chairman of Bethlehem Steel, on a visit to London, called on Sir Ernest Lever (an old friend) to discuss steel industry matters. Over dinner he told Lever that he was extremely concerned about the 'seriously delayed' delivery of an iron-ore carrier being built for Bethlehem on the Clyde. He was convinced in his own mind that 'communist saboteurs' were at work, deliberately impeding completion of the vessel's delivery to America, and he asked Lever whether anything could be done. (This was at a time when McCarthyism was at its height in the States, so the Bethlehem chairman's suspicions were perhaps understandable.)

Lever said that he would arrange for a confidential investigation of the situation on the Clyde to be made. The result of this was that I was despatched to Glasgow the following day to find out all that I could. It was put to me, however, that I was to operate in a totally personal capacity, with neither RTB nor Bethlehem knowing anything (officially) about my journey.

Posing as a freelance journalist from the Commonwealth who was writing an article about the British shipping industry, I duly arrived in Glasgow. I checked unobtrusively with local newspaper offices, talked to the city's mayor and other civic officials, and (more informally) moved round various Glasgow pubs to engage in casual conversation with shipyard workers over a drink. I also got hold of a local boatman to row me down the Clyde so that I could look at the vessel in its entirety from the river, which was not possible from the shore.

It looked to me as if the carrier was clearly nearing completion. I had gleaned virtually nothing of an untoward nature from my earlier conversations with people in the city and so I decided to track down the chairman of the shipbuilding company. It was a Sunday morning by this time, and I was fortunate enough to get hold of him by telephone at his home. He was very amenable and very frank about the iron-carrier's construction programme. Yes, it was behind schedule because of various supply delays, but it would be undertaking its first seagoing trials within a couple of weeks. It was clear from his remarks that there had been no 'Communist sabotage' problems – just plain inability to get the job finished on time. I went back to London straight away, delivering my report on Lever's desk the following morning. He was suitably impressed, apparently, as were the Americans, but the entire incident never featured in RTB's records. It was from such an experience that I learned from a very early stage that a PR operator is expected to undertake almost anything for anybody at any time.

1954

I made my first visit to the USA in the early months of 1954. My assignment was to undertake a detailed study of American television and the use put to it for PR and promotion purposes by leading American steel companies. Commercial TV was on the point of being launched in Britain and nobody – certainly nobody in British Industry – seemed to know very much about it. There was a somewhat naive impression that commercial TV in Britain would operate on very much the same basis as in America.

For most of my time in the States, thanks to arrangements made by Howard Marshall, I was attached to CBS in New York under Edward R. Murrow – a legendary figure, probably America's greatest-ever TV and radio reporter. His weekly TV programmes *See it Now* and *Person to Person*, as well as his daily news commentaries for CBS Radio, commanded immense audiences throughout the States. Part of his job, he remarked to me when I first met him in his CBS office on Madison Avenue, was to interview the great, the near-great, and the relatively unknown.

Although, like everyone else in the TV and radio business in America, he was conscious of the power of programme sponsors (including his own), Murrow was certainly not influenced by the needs of commercialism – the ratings that programmes got or did not get. He stood for the right to present issues and facts as he saw them. 'If I got involved in the ratings business,' he said to me, 'I might be tempted to hot up what I write. And that's something I never want to do.'

I spent several weeks with Murrow, his producer Fred Friendly (another legendary TV figure), and the rest of the Murrow team, watching closely the making of both *See it Now* and *Person to Person*. The first, a weekly 30-minute programme, was sponsored by the Aluminium Corporation of America (Alcoa). Its editorial content, reflecting the week's international news, was left entirely to Murrow. Alcoa had two short commercial breaks in the programme (called 'spots') which were devoted to aluminium products and prepared by their own advertising people. This gave me a first insight into how commercial TV might operate in Britain.

I also spent a good deal of time with the vast US Steel Corporation at its New York headquarters and the nearby TV studios that it used. At that time, as the industry leader, it was spending the dollar equivalent of £1 million per year (£22 million in today's terms) sponsoring a fortnightly play for transmission on Sunday evenings under the title *The United States Steel Hour*. Each play was produced by the prestigious Theatre Guild of New York in close consultation with US Steel itself, who maintained a special unit within its PR department concerned solely with the planning, presentation and promotion of the *Steel Hour*. The best performers available were hired for each production, with US Steel having final oversight over the casting and drawing up of individual players' contracts. In addition, US Steel had two commercial breaks in each programme – between acts of the play being transmitted – for corporate and product sales promotion.

Although the *Steel Hour* was very popular, commanding a regular audience of around 12 million (very high in those days), it seemed clear to me that such close control of the creative side of a drama programme by a sponsor was most unlikely to be allowed in Britain.

Something else, however, was beginning to develop in America that would assuredly be repeated in Britain. This was the effect of violence in TV programmes. It was most noticeable, even in those early days of TV in the States, that violent acts and scenes in many different types of programme were creating a far more serious social problem than TV companies over there were prepared to admit.

As soon as I returned to Britain I was asked to talk to all the embryonic commercial TV programme companies – notably Associated Rediffusion, Associated Broadcasting (ABC), and Granada – then busily starting to set themselves up in various small London offices. I wanted to find out how they proposed to operate, and in particular whether sponsored TV programmes of some sort would be on the cards for companies like RTB. I found that there was a good deal of speculation regarding the latter, and even more important, that there was a dearth of TV production know-how outside the BBC – so much so, in fact, that certain BBC staff were already being poached. In my own case, the fact that I was newly returned from study in the States, the veritable home of commercial TV, resulted in my being offered jobs (rather nebulous jobs, I thought) by all three companies. And when I visited Independent Television News (ITN), then also being set up, the editor, Aidan Crawley, mistakenly assumed that I was a candidate for a TV newsreader's job when I sat down in his office – never mind about the likes of Chris Chataway and Robin Day waiting outside.

It was about this time, too, that Alan Campbell-Johnson asked me to undertake some spare-time research for him in connection with a book about Earl Mountbatten's role as Supreme Commander in South-East Asia (SEAC) in World War II that he was working on.

Campbell-Johnson had served as a member of Mountbatten's staffs in London and the Far East during the war, as well as being his press relations advisor when he was Viceroy of India. His Westminster flat contained a hefty collection of Mountbatten's papers, and my wife Helen and I spent many weekends, over several months, working through them and classifying them.

The papers were a revelation in many respects, at any rate to me. They included private letters from King George VI and other material that has not yet seen the light of day so far as I am aware. One day Mountbatten asked to see us, and I accompanied Campbell-Johnson to his house in Belgravia. We had quite a long discussion with him about his period as Supreme Commander, much of the talk centring on the chain of decisions affecting events in French Indo-China – events which, subsequently and fatefully, led to the Vietnam War many years later. At the end of the discussion Mountbatten turned to me and said: 'Well, Samain, that's what I did and why I did it. Now tell me, what would *you* have done?'

This was, of course, the glorious moment for the man in the street to say his piece, but I don't think I rose very successfully to the occasion.

The interview took place in the library, which he had first entered, rather dramatically, through a hidden door in one of the book-lined walls. We sat in comfortable chairs, surrounded by small tables covered with miniature bejewelled Indian elephants, and drank cocktails served by a footman in blue battledress with the monogram *MofB* embroidered on his breast. When the interview was finished and Mountbatten smilingly started to usher us out, the telephone rang for him. Noel Coward, old friend, was at the other end.

Year Ten: 1958

After eight happy and productive years at RTB I felt the need for a change. Among the various jobs I applied for was one with a company I had never previously heard of named Cementation. I was interviewed by a head-hunter for this job and eventually got it – and so began a task which involved setting up, on an international scale, a PR operation covering the ongoing activities of a mining and civil engineering company which was very skilled in its own field but which, nevertheless, was a company that the outside world had barely heard of, if at all. My work for Cementation was to take me to various parts of the world in a very short space of time – with specific assignments, all of them interesting but in one case very difficult, in Canada, India and Iran.

1959

Cementation was a Doncaster-based company which had prospered during World War II, grown progressively bigger during the post-war years and eventually established an international headquarters on the Albert Embankment in London. Its managing director was a shrewd, friendly Yorkshireman named Cecil Grundy.

Grundy could see the value of good PR, especially in relation to the promotion of Cementation's name and engineering capabilities both in Britain and throughout the world. In addition to setting up a small PR office for him in London, therefore, I soon found myself being dispatched overseas.

My first assignment was in Canada, where Cementation had managed (after others had failed) to sink shafts several hundreds of feet deep on to valuable potash deposits in Saskatchewan, under exceptionally icy weather conditions, employing a special grouting technique for the purpose. I managed to obtain a good deal of publicity for this successful feat in Canadian and United States newspapers, and also elsewhere internationally. It was a good engineering achievement story – good for Cementation and for Britain.

Some months later, however, I was faced with the handling of a very different situation – a very difficult PR issue, in fact. This was in India, where Cementation had landed its biggest contract to date, responsible (as part of a large British engineering consortium) for all civil engineering work involved in the construction of a massive new steelworks being built for the Indian Government at Durgapur, 110 miles north of Calcutta.

The Durgapur site was being carved out of the jungles of Bengal, and a vast army of some 10,000 Indian manual labourers were working on it alongside skilled engineers employing the most modern civil engineering equipment. The entire project, under British control and responsibility, represented something of a prestige race against new steelworks also being built for the Indian Government in two other parts of the country – by German and Russian consortia respectively.

After levelling the Durgapur site, Cementation started work on pile-driving for the foundations. Unfortunately, due to lack of adequate supervision, the Indian labourers involved were driving piles only a few feet into the ground in certain instances – instead of the required 30-40 feet – in order to gain bonus payments for 'completing' their work speedily. Had this fraudulent practice not been discovered by two British engineers (they accidently knocked over the tops of several piles sticking out of the ground during the course of a casual walk across the site one evening) the subsequent consequences would have been calamitous. The placing of a concrete 'raft' on top of such flimsy piling, which in turn would have to support heavy mill machinery, would have resulted in the collapse of the entire structure.

Once the defective work had been detected, a major political problem arose. Cementation was officially blamed for negligence, and various Indian politicians quickly seized upon the incident to accuse Britain of sabotaging India's five-year economic plan. The repercussions rapidly spread to Whitehall and to Cementation in London. The company responded by dispatching to India as many of its specialist engineers throughout the world as it could muster. I, for my part, was told by Grundy to get out to India as fast as possible and 'deal with the press'. That was the total extent of my brief.

I arrived in Calcutta and went up to the site immediately. After that I returned to Calcutta and saw the British High Commissioner there. He left me in no doubt about the political magnitude of the problem, but was most helpful in advising me how to handle the Indian press and, in particular, certain key Indian newspapers. I then went to see the newspaper editors concerned in both Calcutta and Bombay, and also Indian government officials in Delhi. Eventually, beginning with several weeks of defensive talking to all concerned, during which we emphasised Cementation's determination to undertake full remedial work as speedily as possible, the political and press storm finally blew itself out. Cementation did all it could to expedite the necessary corrective work on the steelworks site and generally to put matters right. Its prompt responsive actions saved the day.

On the way home from India I stopped off at Teheran for discussions with the local Cementation management about a more straightforward project. In southern Iran, at Khorramshahr, Cementation had successfully built a bridge in record time (a matter of months), linking the island of Abadan with the mainland. This was a construction achievement for which Cementation naturally wished to take credit and obtain wide-scale publicity. It was also a project in which the Shah had expressed considerable personal interest, with our own Foreign Office following suit.

After discussions with the British ambassador in Teheran, and Paul Masserik, Cementation's Middle East manager, I went with Paul to see His Excellency Jaf'aar Behbehanian, Administrator General of the Royal Estates.

Behbehanian was a man of great influence. He was personally responsible to the Shah for the maintenance and development of the Royal Estates throughout the country, totalling some 20,000 square miles. His powers included the granting of contracts for virtually all types of building on the Royal lands, which included the Abadan-Khorramshahr area. He was clearly a most important person, and he lived surrounded by wealth in a palace of his own on the outskirts of Teheran.

It was an extremely hot day when Paul Masserik and I went to see Behbehanian. We travelled in a Cadillac specially hired by Paul so as to create a suitable impression. We found the marble-pillared corridors of the palace crowded with businessmen and favour-seekers, Western and Iranian, and wondered how long we should have to wait. It became apparent that we had been put at the head of the queue, however, and so we were soon ushered into Behbehanian's lavishly furnished office, where luxurious Persian carpets covered the floor. His desk was at the far end of the room, about sixty feet beyond the tall double doors through which we entered.

As Behbehanian rose from his desk to receive us, a paunchy, powerfully-built man with close-cropped white hair and heavily-lidded eyes, he reminded me strongly of Sidney Greenstreet, the actor renowned for his sinister roles in Hollywood films. It was a feeling that never entirely left me. In conversation he displayed a clear grasp of media matters that I found surprising. He left me in no doubt about the sort of editorial coverage he expected to see in the press in return for the award of construction work to Cementation. It was to help project modern Iran, and it was to be extensive.

When our discussion was over Behbehanian waved his hand with a faintly courteous smile and indicated that we should leave. Paul and I rose from our seats in front of his desk, bowed to him, and walked three paces backwards as protocol demanded. We then turned to start leaving the room, and as we did so we looked straight into the eyes of two hard-looking young Iranians who were certainly not in the room when we entered it. They were sitting some ten feet behind us, their hands on shoulder-holsters inside their jackets. They got to their feet as we began walking and followed us. When we reached the double-doors at the far end of the room we found that they were locked and we could not get out. Behbehanian immediately unlocked them by means of a remote control button on his desk – apologising as he did so. We learned later that he was terrified of assassination. The two young men following us (we also later learned) were agents of Savak, the state secret police.

Back in London, with Foreign Office support, I managed to obtain a good deal of worldwide press publicity for the successful building of the Khorramshahr Bridge by Cementation. And the British press did us proud, too. It was a good 'export' story and they were quite keen on getting hold of industrial stories featuring British engineering successes overseas at that time. As regards Behbehanian, I neither saw nor heard of him again.

1960

Early in 1960 I received a totally unexpected invitation to join the Ford Motor Company in Britain as head of public relations. I was to succeed the famous Colonel Maurice Buckmaster, wartime controller of agents dropped into France to aid the Resistance. He had worked for Ford for a total of some 30 years, both before and after the war, and he wanted to retire.

Sir Patrick Hennessy, chairman of Ford of Britain, offered me the job. I gathered that he had made some private enquiries about me and decided that I was his man. He was a formidable character, of medium height, sandy-haired, grave and unsmiling in manner. His pale-blue eyes would suddenly glitter imperiously. A world-class figure in the motor industry, it was said that whenever he dealt with the parent Ford company in Detroit he only talked to Henry Ford II – and that Henry only talked to God.

'How much do you know about cars?' Sir Patrick asked me during our first interview.

'Absolutely nothing', I said. 'I can't tell you anything about what goes on beneath the bonnet. I'm very much Mr Average Motorist.' Sir Patrick nevertheless took me on.

A great deal has been written about the Ford Motor Company as it was in those far-off days – its undoubted brilliance in designing and producing cars on an enormous scale for mass markets, its marketing and promotional skills, but above all, perhaps, about its then long-standing and deep-seated labour problems. Bad labour relations were by no means uncommon in those days, of course, but in Ford's case they were undoubtedly exacerbated by the sheer size of the main manufacturing site at Dagenham, where 55,000 people worked and 27 trade unions represented them. In 1960, cars at Dagenham were being produced at a rate of 3,000 a day – 1,000 of them best-selling Anglias. Tensions throughout the plant under such high-pressure conditions were perhaps inevitable. I noted, on more than one occasion, that strikes emerged for reasons quite unconnected with the 'official' reasons for grievance. The biggest source of trouble seemed to be the re-timing of one particular operation or another on the production line. In one case, as I saw for myself, a time-and-motion-study man altered, on the spot, the time allowed for fixing an Anglia windscreen in position from 10.75 to 10 seconds per unit. The men at work on this operation threw down their tools in disgust and walked off the job. They were immediately followed by their mates further down the line and within a matter of hours the management had to start laying off hundreds, and ultimately thousands, of other workers on the Dagenham plant because of the disruption caused by the windscreen re-timing decision. In sum, therefore, an incident involving six men at 11 a.m. one morning had escalated to a total shutdown of large areas of the Dagenham site, affecting some 20,000 men, by 3 p.m. the same afternoon.

Ford made strenuous efforts in subsequent years to overcome their labour relations problems, and eventually they made real progress. It took a very long time, however, for the inherent bitterness at Dagenham to subside. Memories of pre-war days, when trade unions were prohibited and the works police had excessive disciplinary powers – including on-the-spot dismissal powers for minor infractions – lingered for many years. The only reason why men worked for Ford in the 1930s was the high pay Ford offered when jobs were available – £5 a week on average, the highest rate in the London area.

It was not long before I met Henry Ford II on one of his periodic visits to England. A plump, expensively-suited man, he was always superficially polite, although one had a very definite feeling that an iron will lurked beneath his courteous exterior. 'Don't risk his knowledge,' Sir Patrick Hennessy warned me before I met him. 'You will find that Mr Ford knows all about your department and its operations.' And he did.

One night during his English visit he telephoned me at my home in Essex at about 11 p.m., just as I was entering the front door after a particularly long day. I was feeling somewhat tired, and the incessant ring of the phone was irksome. 'Is that Bryan Samain?' American voice No.1 asked with quiet urgency.

'Yes,' I said.

There was silence for a full 30 seconds before anything further happened. Then American voice No. 2 chipped in: 'Mr Ford will shortly speak to you.'

Half a minute later the great man himself finally came on. 'Say, I wonder, do you know where Leo Beebe is?'

At that precise moment, Leo Beebe, who was one of Henry Ford's top aides, could have been anywhere in the world – in any one of around twenty separate Ford locations. 'I'll certainly try to find him, Mr Ford,' I said.

'I'd be glad if you would. Call me here at Grosvenor House by 8 a.m. Thank you. Goodnight.'

It's always more difficult, of course (or certainly was in those days without benefit of a mobile), to attempt an international telephone search late at night from one's home rather than an office. However, thanks to some helpful Ford switchboard operators in various parts of the world, I finally tracked Leo Beebe's last known movements down to a business address in Paris. 'He left a while ago for Detroit,' one of them informed me. 'I understand he got on a plane at Orly airport.'

By this time my news-hunting blood was up. I was determined to squeeze the last scintilla of fact concerning Leo Beebe's homeward journeying from wherever I could squeeze it. I rang British Airways. With their prompt assistance I ascertained not only Beebe's Detroit-bound flight number and estimated time of arrival, but also his plane's probable longitude and latitude position over the Atlantic at the precise time I was making my enquiry. Armed with this information I then rang Henry Ford at Grosvenor House. He briefly acknowledged all that I had to say, and that was that. (From where I was it had taken some three hours of telephone calls to track Beebe's movements, and by this time I didn't really know, and frankly didn't care, whether I was dragging Henry from his bed to give him the news.)

'He probably did all that to try you out,' remarked Sir Patrick drily when I told him the following morning.

A few weeks later I met Henry Ford's principal lieutenant, Robert MacNamara, then president of Ford Motors, who later became US Defence Secretary and ultimately President of the World Bank. He was paying a flying visit to London.

MacNamara was an entirely different type of man. Tall, slim, business-like and quietly brisk, he breezed in and out of London in 24 hours. He had a mind like a computer and made little or no impact – on me, at any rate.

The year 1960 was dominated, for Ford of Britain, by the acquisition of total ownership of the company by the US Ford parent.

For many years Ford of Detroit had owned just 54 per cent of Ford of Britain, the remainder of the shares being held by members of the public. The parent Ford Company now wanted to buy these shares, for which it made a handsome offer – £7.25 for each £1 Ordinary share. The total value of the American bid was £128.5 million (£2.51

billion at today's values), making it the biggest bid of the kind up to that time.

Close secrecy surrounded the launching of the bid, which was announced by the board of Ford of Britain in London on a Monday afternoon. As part of the security arrangements, all the directors, together with the company secretary and myself, were locked in the Ford flat in Grosvenor House from the early morning onwards. We stayed there until the bid announcement was made via the Stock Exchange at 3.30 p.m.

The news of the bid initially sparked an enormous wave of public reaction, much of it angry and critical. The *Daily Express* for example, immediately decided to mount a strong campaign against the very idea – even though the proprietor of the *Express*, Lord Beaverbrook, was a close personal friend of Sir Patrick Hennessey – the two often holidayed together at Beaverbrook's holiday villa in the South of France. Max Aitken, Beaverbrook's son, a Battle of Britain hero who now worked for his father, called upon Hennessey and informed him that, despite personal friendships, the *Express* was going to attack the bid strongly. The idea of American Ford acquiring Ford of Britain in toto was like someone trying to filch the Crown Jewels from the Tower of London.

The feelings aroused did not end there, either. The House of Commons debated the matter – the only time, it was said, that such an issue had ever been an official subject of debate in Parliament. As a result, I found myself taking up station for several hours one afternoon in a room made available to me in the Commons – to act as a temporary information centre for MPs of all parties who suddenly wanted loads of facts and figures about Ford's activities and operations in Britain. After talking to me they returned to the chamber to resume the debate, better informed as some of them certainly needed to be.

Within a few weeks, however, the Ford Transaction (as the government coyly referred to it) had faded from the parliamentary scene and from the headlines. Ford's American parent acquired all the outstanding shares it was after and duly paid for them. Life carried on at Dagenham as if nothing had happened. On the PR side, we resumed more normal activities.

A typical promotional 'stunt' organised by my PR team at that time took place at Goodwood. It was designed to re-focus press and public attention on the Ford Anglia's performance power and reliability – to help maintain the Anglia's pre-eminent sales appeal. Three teams of expert drivers – each comprising a racing driver (Jack Brabham was one of them), a leading rally motorist, and a national press motoring correspondent – were booked to drive three Anglia cars, one per team, round the Goodwood track continuously for seven days and nights, each car racking up 10,000 miles non-stop in the process. The Anglias performed perfectly in the event, and Ford gained widespread publicity for an impressive endurance test. It was one of those occasions when absolutely nothing went wrong.

1961

The following year two new Ford cars were launched – the Classic and the Capri. Behind the scenes, unusually, there were mixed opinions about the likely strength of their appeal to the market. One of Dagenham's senior car sales executives, a veteran of many launches, privately expressed the view that the Classic was such a problematic car that it ought to be buried in someone's garden and forgotten about. Nobody seemed to know what to make of the Capri, either, until Sir Patrick Hennessey finally pronounced that it was to be marketed as a 'two-person personal car'.

Launching a new model is never easy. Marketing and publicity plans require highly imaginative flair and (equally important) to be executed with great precision and skill. Everything has to be arranged under conditions of great secrecy, so that nothing is publicly revealed until 'launching day'. This means, among other things, that hundreds of new cars have to be driven all over the country in advance and strictly 'under wraps' so as to reach the dealers' showrooms in good time without being seen. The entire launch has to be backed by massive advertising, and this also has to be prepared as secretly as possible. Inevitably, there are times when advance details of a new model are in danger of being 'leaked' by someone to the media, which can result (and has done so on more than one occasion) in an interim injunction being sought and applied against the newspaper concerned.

The new Classic and Capri were both given the usual large-scale send-off, complete with glossy fanfares of wide-ranging press and publicity. (Television was not much of an option in those days. It was a very new medium, and I heard more than one advertising man say that TV in Britain would never, ever, sell a single motor car.)

The Classic was introduced first. It was unveiled to the press at Brands Hatch, where motoring correspondents were given the customary opportunity to try out the new car and show off their driving skills at the same time. Also in accordance with custom, the head of Ford PR was expected to lead correspondents round the first single lap of the Brands Hatch circuit – which I did, cautiously, as I was quite happy to let my press friends outshine me.

When I finally appeared on the home straight of the final circuit, still driving at a steady pace, a deep-throated cheer went up from those members of the press who were still waiting their turn. I was driving at 40 mph, probably the only person ever to drive round Brands Hatch in so modest a manner; but I was, after all, Mr Average Motorist.

It was shortly after this time, too, that Ford launched its new Transit van, destined to be a best seller for very many years. The promotional theme was 'Hold Everything' and the press introduction was held at the Connaught Rooms in Holborn – booked on account of the Rooms' vast size and accommodation capability. Despite these advantages, however, a very large hole had to be hacked out of the rear wall of the building so that we could get the Transit van inside. (I have often wondered if it is still there – and whether it's proved of any use to subsequent Connaught Rooms clients.)

I inherited a number of other rather unexpected responsibilities when I joined Ford. There was the Ford Motor Works Band, for instance, which was as competent and as enjoyable to listen to as any of the great brass bands of the North – and, like them, undertook performances all over the country. The bandmaster used to come and see me once or twice a year to discuss his tour plans for the band and also get his annual budget agreed. Otherwise I never had any contact with him. (The band, I believe, ceased to exist some years later, as part of a cost-cutting drive.)

Then there were the factory guides. Every day, weekends excepted, there were two conducted tours of Dagenham, designed to show how Ford cars were made, available free of charge to members of the public provided they could make their own travelling arrangements. The tours had been run for many years and were exceedingly popular. There was never any shortage of applications from the public and they provided, in my view, down-to-earth PR in the most practical sense.

Looking after the factory guides who conducted these daily tours was another of my responsibilities. There were

17 of them, if I remember correctly, and they were drawn from a variety of backgrounds. I accompanied several of them on one or two of their daily public tours to see how they were run, and how they got on with the public. I was impressed by what I saw, but I did not feel they were adequately paid for all that they did. So I arranged a modest rise in their wages. To my pleasant surprise they later presented me with an engraved tankard which I still have to this day. It is the only time I have been so rewarded.

The biggest of my unexpected responsibilities was supervising Ford of Britain's participation in international rallies. It was something I had not discussed with Sir Patrick on joining – in fact it was never mentioned. 'It's really not my field at all,' I pointed out to him some time later.

'Not mine either,' replied Sir Patrick. 'Just keep getting results, that's what we need.'

Fortunately I had on my PR staff a first-class rally competition manager named Edgell Fabris. He had been running the admin side of Ford's participation in international rallies for years. He could tell, by careful study of the rules and conditions governing any particular rally event, whether or not Ford stood a chance of winning a prize. And he was generally right.

One thing I learned very quickly was that success in a major rally invariably resulted in soaring sales for the type of car that had been driven. When Ford won the Ladies' Prize in the Monte Carlo rally, for instance, sales of the Anglia zoomed upwards – especially in Europe.

One overseas international rally in which Ford scored notable successes during the 1950s, notably with the Ford Zephyr, was the East African Safari Rally, a gruelling 4,500 mile event for drivers and cars alike. First held in 1953, it was still relatively new and unknown to the public in Europe. In publicity terms therefore, it needed a strong shot in the arm to achieve widespread headline attention. To get it more extensively publicised I arranged for Courtenay Edwards, one of the leading motoring writers of the day and a former *Daily Mail* motoring correspondent, to cover the Safari for one year entirely at Ford's expense – irrespective of results and whether or not in Ford's favour. The resultant news stories that Courtenay wrote and placed in various British and European newspapers certainly succeeded in making the Safari better known.

I did not spend too long a period with Ford Britain – less than two years, in fact – as I had very mixed feelings about the company. In many ways it was highly efficient, but in human terms it was not so. I felt, as did others, that the rigid systems and procedures of the US parent company did not help. Their exclusive priority, it always seemed to me, it was cars, trucks and tractors constantly flowing off their production lines, with little regard for the people who made them.

American executives were constantly visiting Dagenham. On one fairly typical day that I can recall, 164 visitors arrived from Detroit and fanned out across the plant in all directions, combing and checking through operational plans and figures. This did not make for good relations and among other things, undoubtedly contributed towards the voluntary departure, a couple of years later, of a number of key British executives.

I left Ford to rejoin Howard Marshall at RTB with few regrets, carrying with me a clear memory of one colleague with whom I had always worked particularly well. He was John Read, at that time Ford's director of car sales. I was to meet him again, in greatly changed circumstances, ten years later.

1962

When I returned to RTB it was to act as Howard Marshall's deputy. This really meant running his department on a day-to-day basis as he had become a rather sick man who was hardly able to come into the office at all.

There was an immense PR project to be undertaken on my return, namely planning and organising the official opening of Spencer steelworks and strip mill, then in the final stages of construction at Llanwern, near Newport in South Wales. One of the most advanced plants of its kind in Europe, it was designed to produce some 2 million tons of steel sheet and coil a year. Its design also embodied the first use of a computer for complete control of a hot strip mill – the heart of the entire works operation. (The computer set-up was installed in a building the size of a three-bedroom house alongside the mill. 'In 30 years' time,' a computer expert told me on the site one day, 'the march of technology will enable the enormous amount of gear in that building to be so miniaturised that it will fit into a small suitcase.' It was a most accurate prophesy, as we now all know.)

The works was being built on an area of 'rotten land' (poor farmland) covering nearly four miles in length and over one and a half miles in width. It was the biggest civil engineering project of the kind ever undertaken in Britain up to that time. McAlpine were the main contractors, and some 400 sub-contractors were also involved. The original estimated cost was £80 million (£1.45 billion at today's values), but the eventual cost soared to £140 million (£2.53 billion today).

The official opening was set for 25 October 1962. The Queen and the Duke of Edinburgh had agreed to open the plant. A total of 1500 VIP guests were to be invited, including several cabinet ministers in Macmillan's government together with the chairmen of leading steel and industrial companies (plus their wives) from all over the world.

The planning of the entire event, for which I was the co-ordinator, took several months. Detailed arrangements had to be agreed with dozens of officials (including, of course, the Royal equerries at Buckingham Palace). Travelling schedules had to be established and special trains booked to carry many of the guests to and from London. Large marquees had to be hired and erected for catering and general reception purposes. The entire affair was rather like a major film production.

One of the small team working with me on the planning and preparation work was the late Earl of Gosford, at that time a special consultant to RTB. He was a former Lord-in-waiting at Buckingham Palace and he had also been a junior minister at the Foreign Office. His knowledge and advice were most helpful. At one stage, when various details regarding the start of the Royal tour were being considered (the 'start' being at a remote end of the vast steelworks site), a serious concern arose in the minds of certain RTB directors that suitable toilet facilities might need to be made available to the Queen on her arrival. The matter increasingly worried them, and they even considered the possibility of constructing a special facility to be substantially built in brick and stone for security reasons. In the end, John Gosford rang the palace to make discreet enquiries about Her Majesty's arrangements. He spoke to his friend, Sir Michael Adeane, HM's private secretary. 'Tell them not to worry, old boy,' Adeane breezily replied. 'The Queen always arrives at public events ready to go straight into action.'

Security was, of course, a major consideration in planning the official opening, but there was virtually no way of completely protecting the Llanwern site at that time, with its largely unguarded perimeter covering many acres of rough farmland. Some weeks before the opening, the site was inspected by representatives of both the local police and MI5 who apparently felt confident that adequate cover could be provided. In the event, the entire day passed off without mishap. In fact it was a very considerable success and the works was well and truly launched, with excellent publicity both at home and overseas in the press and on TV.

The works was originally called Spencer Works, named after RTB's then managing director, a remarkable man named Henry Spencer who was the driving force behind the entire project – closely aided by Campbell Adamson, the works General Manager (later Sir Campbell Adamson, Director-General of the CBI and Chairman of Abbey National). Spencer duly received a knighthood for his services to the steel industry, but he died in 1964. Had he lived, however, he would have probably been made (in the opinion of many) the first chairman of the British Steel Corporation when it was formed following full nationalisation of the industry in 1967.

A few weeks after the opening of Spencer Works (later renamed Llanwern Works) RTB found itself involved in a very unusual take-over battle. The independently owned Whitehead Iron and Steel Co., located at Newport, was an important customer for steel billets – used for re-rolling into a variety of steel products – from RTB's Redbourn Works in Lincolnshire. The relationship between the two companies, in fact, was long-standing and close.

To the surprise of RTB, and no doubt Whitehead as well, the major steel producer Stewarts and Lloyds (S & L), based at Corby in Northamptonshire, suddenly announced a bid for Whiteheads. S & L's own range of products included billets, and it wanted to secure Whitehead as an outlet for them. The loss of Whitehead's business to RTB would have been serious, representing some 10 per cent of RTB's total turnover. RTB therefore decided to counter-bid, and the stage was thereby set for a struggle between a large private sector steel company (S & L) and the only steel company (RTB) then owned by the state.

For the battle to be fought at all, however, RTB would need Treasury support, and this (surprisingly to some) was duly forthcoming. Knowledgeable people in the City felt, nevertheless, that RTB could not possibly win: the Treasury would be too slow, it was argued, to make up its mind and move quickly enough to satisfy the market. In this the doubters were proved wrong. The Treasury set up a special small working group comprising some of its own senior officials and key RTB directors (including Sir Henry Spencer) which met daily and almost continuously until the end. As S & L progressively increased its offer, so the Treasury rapidly responded with a higher counter-offer. After a few days the Stock Exchange suspended dealings in Whitehead shares, but by then the battle was virtually won. The big City institutions threw in their lot with the Treasury and RTB – and the last (crucial) block of shares was voted in RTB's favour by Sir Edwin McAlpine, a personal friend of Henry Spencer. (This final moment had its own small element of drama, with Spencer hurriedly trying to reach McAlpine by telephone whilst the latter was sunning himself on a holiday beach in the South of France.)

Howard Marshall and I sat in on most of the Treasury/RTB meetings that took place during those hectic few days, so that we could deal with financial press and industrial correspondents who were urgently following the proceedings. It was an instructive, unique business: a Conservative government and a nationalised steel company joining together, for the first and probably the only time, to fight a private sector company in the City's market-place.

1967

Other than the Royal opening of Spencer/Llanwern Works and the Whitehead takeover battle, the years 1962–1966 were comparatively uneventful for me at RTB – until I was seconded from my PR job to undertake marketing and sales work for the company in South Wales. This led to my gaining, entirely unexpectedly, an unusual sidelight on the conduct of the Vietnam War.

In the early autumn of 1967, when I was temporarily acting as a divisional sales manager for a number of RTB products, ranging from stainless steel to sheet metal pressings and pre-painted steel sheet, I was selected to join a small (and apparently hand-picked) British sales delegation. Our mission was to proceed to Washington, under the auspices of the British Government, to attend a highly secret briefing in the Pentagon regarding the US Armed Forces' material supply requirements for the war in Vietnam. My own membership of the delegation arose from the fact that the varied RTB steel products in my sales 'portfolio' included ammunition boxes, manufactured in different shapes and sizes at a small RTB pressworks in Swansea.

Together with 10 representatives from other British companies, some of them very well known, and all of them offering products of possible military interest to the US authorities, I arrived in Washington one September evening. We were accompanied by a representative of Army Sales from the Ministry of Defence, having previously been security-cleared and vouched for back in London by the UK Government. On arrival in Washington we were immediately briefed in detail by British Embassy staff as to how the Pentagon meeting would be held and what it would cover. The background to all this was that the UK Government was trying to obtain a stronger footing for British industry in the highly competitive US defence market. Our delegation was the first to be invited to Washington by the US authorities, and it was hoped that others would follow.

The following day we duly went to the Pentagon. Stringent security was in force there, as we expected, with the personal credentials of each one of us carefully vetted by US military personnel 'reception staff' (male and female) before we were allowed to enter the building. Every one of us had our wrists stamped with a code number – which could only be revealed under ultra-violet light – and the code number was changed each day.

The briefings lasted three days. They took place in a very large meeting hall and were attended by 500 people, most of them representatives of US industrial corporations. There were also representatives of Canadian firms present, as well as ourselves.

No note-taking of any kind was permitted at any of the briefings, and burly US Marine guards walked up and down the aisles to ensure that this instruction was in no way breached. The various presentations by senior US Army officers, dealing with weapons and munitions of all kinds, were detailed and secret. The Vietnam War had been going on for three years (unknown to any of us at the time, of course, it still had eight more years to run) and the Kennedy Administration was strongly increasing the US military presence in the country. It did not take much working out that the Americans, as well as seeking munitions and equipment supplies at keen prices, were also keen to get new ideas.

This was borne out when a middle-aged Army general addressed us and gave his own opinion. 'Gentlemen,' he said, 'my grandfather fought the Indians with very primitive weapons – sometimes even using bows and arrows like the Indians themselves. We face a similar enemy in Vietnam, used to living off the land and experts in fighting will o' the wisp guerrilla-style warfare. I think we need to find new, unconventional means of fighting the Vietnam War ourselves – so if anyone here has got any ideas for new products, we'd be glad to have them.'

So far as I am aware, there were no British representatives present at the briefings who could effectively respond to the US general's plea. All of us were offering, and hoping to sell, conventional equipment. And the extraordinary thing to me was that the US military seemed to recognise the sort of tactics they needed to employ in Vietnam but simply failed to employ them. They continued to use, until the war was brought to its bitter end, so-called 'blanket' techniques involving mass indiscriminate bombings and large-scale defoliation of the land, resulting in the complete obliteration of vast tracts of forest across the country.

I did not succeed in selling any ammunition boxes to the US military in Washington: their delivery and price requirements were hopelessly unattractive. But I returned to Britain a good deal wiser about a war in which a small south-east Asian country was tying down a superpower with obvious success.

Back in the UK, the steel industry was fast becoming dominated by the prospect, for the second time within 20 years, of wholesale nationalisation and organisational change. The Labour Government under Harold Wilson was determined to press forward with placing the entire industry under state ownership – so that steel, like coal, electricity and gas before it, would give Labour full control, in Wilson's words, of the commanding heights of the economy.

The operation would be an enormous one. Excluding RTB (the only company not de-nationalised when the Conservatives returned to power in 1951) some 13 major steel companies would once again be wrested from private ownership. The lives of 270,000 people working in the industry would be affected.

To prepare and plan for the change-over, the government set up a high-level Organising Committee, comprising both civil servants and the chairmen of the various companies involved, including RTB. Once re-nationalisation began in the autumn of 1967, the reorganisation was put into immediate effect. The companies were drawn together, overnight, into four main regional groups covering England, Scotland and Wales. RTB, together with the Steel Company of Wales and Guest Keen Iron & Steel Co. Ltd, comprised the South Wales Group. This alone involved 70,000 employees in works and offices extending from Newport in the east to Llanelli in West Wales. It also embraced three very large steelworks and strip mills – at Ebbw Vale, Llanwern (Newport) and Port Talbot.

The new chairman of the South Wales Group was Fred Cartwright, formerly chairman of the Steel Company of Wales. He was based, together with a small headquarters staff, at the Port Talbot plant. He rang me up soon after taking charge and asked me to join him as head of information services for the Group (I was living with my family in Cardiff at the time). I took up my new job shortly afterwards and, as I had known him fairly well for several years, we soon struck up an effective relationship.

A distinguished mechanical engineer by profession, Cartwright was a highly experienced steelman who had been a leading figure behind the building of the Port Talbot strip mill in 1951. He was no doubt Conservative by political inclination, but at the same time he was essentially practical and positive in his attitude towards re-nationalisation and the efficiency benefits he felt it could bring. He was under the clear impression at the time, as were others, that the four regional groups of the British

Steel Corporation (as the new set-up was now named) would be autonomous – operating quite independently of each other, with scope for relative freedom of action leading to greater efficiencies.

This concept of autonomy, however, was soon rudely shattered by BSC in London, where a large, growing headquarters was already springing up. Based to begin with in offices in Kingsway, the London headquarter staffs swelled rapidly in size, settling eventually in an imposing building in Victoria, alongside the National Coal Board's equally imposing HQ next door. Even more ominous, it soon became apparent that none of the regional groups, from their chairmen downwards, could do very much without reference to London. In my own case, so far as relations with the press were concerned, I was told that I could not communicate directly with national newspapers, only local ones. Anything of potential national press interest arising within my group was to be handed over to London, to be dealt with by the central PR and press staff there.

As well as the considerable number of existing administrative managers and staffs already being drafted into the new BSC headquarters, new arrivals from outside the industry had also taken up office – including Lord Melchett, the first chairman, who came from the City, and Will Camp, from the Gas Council, who was appointed director of information services. There was also a prominent trades union figure, with no previous experience of the steel industry or its unions, who had appeared as director of labour relations. (Lord Melchett died a few years later. Will Camp, a highly political person, proved too controversial in the job and was eventually fired.)

My outstanding impression of BSC was that from its earliest days it was excessively bureaucratic and committee-ridden, involving frequent and time-wasting visits to

London – utterly frustrating, restrictive and unrewarding. So far as I was concerned, it was time to move on.

Year Twenty: 1968

I left the steel industry early in 1968 to take up PR work in a more promising field. I joined Richard Costain Ltd as head of PR in London, at their headquarters near Waterloo Station.

Costain, I soon found, was a remarkably progressive and thrustful civil engineering and construction company. It had its origins in Liverpool, its driving force for many years being Sir Richard Costain. Under his command the company expanded greatly in the south in the 1920s and 30s, building thousands of houses in the Greater London area, notably in Croydon and South Hornchurch. It also completed, by the outbreak of the Second World War, the large Dolphin Square apartment complex facing the Thames in south-west London. During the war itself the company constructed airfields, ordnance factories and other military works all over the country.

By all accounts Sir Richard Costain was a colourful character – a captain of industry who became a tycoon. He died some years before I joined the company, but many stories were still told about him. One of the favourites, arising at a time when Costain was gaining more and more overseas business shortly after the war, concerned a visit by Sir Richard to South America to negotiate a major civil engineering contract. This led to Costain's purchase of the Stafford Hotel in St James – simply because no other way could be found of accommodating the considerable number of important clients whom Sir Richard wished to bring over to London. When first informed of the problem by cable, he crisply replied: 'Buy a hotel.'

(When I was working for Ford Motor Company I frequently used the Stafford Hotel for entertainment purposes. On one occasion my guest was the then editor of the *Financial Times*, the distinguished journalist Gordon Newton. 'Good of you to bring me here,' he remarked. This is where Cabinet ministers also bring me when they want to leak something.')

From the 1960s onwards Costain succeeded in landing a series of prestigious civil contracts in the Middle East, notably in the Gulf state of Dubai. These included the building of Dubai's international airport and the construction of a large harbour for sea-going shipping. The value of the harbour contract was £24 million (the equivalent of £352 million today).

The Dubai contracts were awarded by The Ruler of Dubai, the late Sheikh Rashid. His personal representative in the UK was Mahdi Al Tajir, a highly trusted advisor who held the title of director of The Ruler's affairs and with whom Costain primarily dealt. Sheikh Rashid was then head of the Al Maktoum family in Dubai and the inspirational force behind the transformation of Dubai itself from a small, sleepy collection of Arab settlements overlooking Dubai Creek into the great modern city and Middle East commercial hub that it is today.

Mahdi Al Tajir, whom I met and dealt with on frequent occasions, had an extraordinary career. Born in Bahrain and educated at a grammar school in Lancashire, he was originally appointed head of Customs by The Ruler and thereafter greatly progressed in his service. He became one of the world's wealthiest men, owning estates and properties in Scotland, London, mainland Europe and elsewhere.

He was a hard taskmaster, but Costain met the standards of performance that he expected. In my own case, he certainly proved demanding in his publicity expectations. Dubai at the time was a largely unknown state – completely unknown, in fact, to Fleet Street editors, some of whom had never even heard of it.

On one occasion, when he was ready to sign a contract with Costain directors at the large country house and estate that he then owned in Sunningdale, Tajir let it be known that he was expecting a full turn-out by the national press to witness the signing at 9 a.m. the following morning. I of course knew (but felt it undiplomatic to mention) that the press would certainly not be prepared to travel 25 miles out of London at such an early hour and for such an event. I therefore arranged for my entire PR and publicity department, some 12 people, to turn up at Sunningdale shortly before the appointed hour to 'represent' various national newspapers. We took a company photographer along with us for good measure and it looked, all in all, a reasonably impressive press party. Afterwards, with the help of some friendly contacts on certain Fleet Street newspapers, we got some decent coverage.

Later, I was able to arrange for the publication of a special Dubai supplement in *The Times*, and for similar editorial features to be placed elsewhere. I like to think, looking back, that I helped to make Dubai better known and more firmly placed in the public mind.

1970

Towards the end of 1969, whilst still working for Costain, I received a totally unexpected telephone call from John Read, whom I had worked with at Ford Motor Company ten years earlier. I knew that he had left Ford to join EMI some time in the 1960s – and I also knew that he had recently been made EMI's chief executive. It came as a complete surprise to me, nevertheless, when he invited me to his Manchester Square office to talk to him about the possibility of joining EMI as head of public relations.

This was to be an entirely new appointment – no one had ever been asked to handle PR for the EMI Group on a global basis before. It all sounded very exciting, and so it proved to be. EMI was engaged in a spread of businesses ranging from music, films and entertainment to commercial and military electronics – a challenging spread, with some areas (notably music) much more strongly identified with EMI than others.

When I joined the group in March 1970 I found that everything had to be started from scratch. There was not even a piece of paper describing EMI's various worldwide activities and interests in concise terms. Over the next few weeks I moved round the Group to learn about what went on at various key centres – Abbey Road, the record-pressing factory and a whole clutch of electronics factories at Hayes, Middlesex, among them. I also visited various other parts of the Group – including Elstree Film Studios, The Blackpool Tower Company, and Thames Television (in which EMI had a controlling interest).

John Read gave me strong support from the outset. He had succeeded the legendary Sir Joseph Lockwood as chief executive, Sir Joseph remaining as chairman – a post he had occupied since 1954, when, at the age of 50 and a flour-miller by profession, he had been persuaded to join the ailing Electric & Musical Industries Ltd, as the company was then known. He saved it from bankruptcy in his first week (borrowing money from the City to pay the wages bill) and saw it grow under his leadership to become, as he once described it to me, Britain's most glamorous business.

Read proved even more dynamic at EMI than I had known him to be at Ford. He recruited a small number of seasoned executives to reinforce his somewhat lean headquarters staff at Manchester Square and drove EMI forward with increasing success over the next few years, despite occasional setbacks. Equipped with a clear, analytical mind and powers of rapid decision, he was also a very effective communicator. A grammar school boy who made his way upwards through sheer brains and hard work, I always thought (and still do) that in his day he was one of the best examples of meritocracy that Britain had produced.

With its spread of interests and diverse range of activities across the world, EMI had (inevitably, perhaps) an extremely diverse group of distinguished and colourful personalities within its organisation. Prominent among these was the famous impresario Bernard Delfont (later Lord Delfont), head of EMI's entertainment operations. Others who sat on the main board as non-executive directors included Sir Ian Jacob, distinguished former soldier and sometime director-general of the BBC; and Lord Shawcross, one of the outstanding lawyers of his day, and chief British prosecutor at the Nuremberg war crimes trials. There were many other well-known people working for EMI, too, some of whom are mentioned later in these pages.

I first met Bernard Delfont in his lime-panelled office in Golden Square. He was sitting at his desk smoking his customary cigar, talking at the same time into two of the five white telephones on his desk. 'Come in, come in,' he beckoned to me, putting his hand over one of the telephones and laying the other down as he spoke. 'I've got a lovely deal going here.' He nodded towards the phones, and in one sentence he epitomised himself as the fast-dealing entrepreneur and showman that he undoubtedly was.

It was most refreshing, for me, to find EMI's directors and top managers generally sensitive to PR needs, ready in particular to respond to press enquiries. This was in sharp contrast to some of my earlier experiences in other companies, where it was often difficult to get executives and others to meet the press – let alone address themselves to any looming public relations issue. 'We will always give an answer,' John Read was fond of saying. And Bernard Delfont himself, unlike many businessmen, actually liked the press and counted several journalists as his friends. 'I know what they want and what they need. I understand them,' he would add.

One of my first problems at EMI was to find some means of describing the nature and range of its businesses in simple and hopefully memorable terms. For years EMI had been briefly described notably in the City, as 'The Beatles Company' and this was plainly not good enough. I managed to get John Read and all the executive directors round a table one day to agree on a short, descriptive sentence covering the EMI Group. After considerable argument and discussion the line agreed by all present was 'International Leaders in Music, Electronics and Leisure' – a line to be badged on all stationery, record labels and other products, vehicles and anywhere else where signage was required. It was not the most dynamic of descriptions or slogans, but it was a start.

The fast-moving environment that was EMI in those days was one in which events sometimes moved too quickly. One day in 1970 Cliff Michelmore and his friend Gordon Reece walked into John Read's office with a proposal to set up, with EMI's help, an audio-visual company aimed at creating programmes for video cassettes and establishing a presence in the vast new market that was envisaged. John Read bought the idea, although (as it turned out) the video cassette 'revolution' had yet to arrive and was in fact several years away. A new subsidiary company, EMI Audio Visual Services, was immediately formed, generating a surprising amount of publicity as soon as it was announced, probably on account of the fact that the well known TV personality Cliff Michelmore was involved. It took quite a time, however, for the new company to start making and selling video cassettes (and then only of the sponsored business documentary variety): the company was, in short, one that had started its life rather too early.

1970 was also the year that EMI formed a joint company with MGM for film production, and also a second joint company to manage Elstree Film Studios – MGM having closed its nearby studios at Borehamwood. These arrangements took place when Bryan Forbes was running Elstree and had embarked on a major programme of film production for EMI which had been heralded, with great optimism at the time, as the 'white hope' revival of the British film industry. The joining of EMI with MGM would greatly reinforce the Elstree programme, it was felt, and indeed resulted in a number of successful films, notably Joseph Losey's *The Go Between* and *Get Carter* starring Michael Caine. The link with MGM was not to last very long, however, and the Bryan Forbes programme also came to an early end.

The largest single element of EMI's worldwide activities was, as it had always been, the making and marketing of recorded music. EMI had established a pre-eminent position from its earliest days in 1898, when one of its predecessor companies, The Gramophone Company, was formed. It was imbued on the one hand with the strong classical traditions of His Master's Voice (around whose trade mark, familiarly known as the Dog and Trumpet, a separate mythology still persists) and on the other with the frenetic competitiveness of the pop music business. The latter was something that I never really came to terms with, any more than a good many other people of my generation; but pop contributed 90 per cent of EMI's music profits. It was also a business where a hit song could seemingly generate a fortune for somebody, literally overnight. (A flop, of course, could see big money invested disappear just as quickly.)

I must confess that I was always half-fascinated by the skill of the people I called 'tasters', young men and women who spent all their working days (and perhaps nights) listening to pop 'demo' tapes sent in to EMI by unknown hopefuls – newly formed bands and/or singers who had launched themselves in a burst of usually noisy hopefulness. The 'tasters' were people gifted, according to those in the know, with 'golden ears': they could often spot a potential hit within seconds. Those not endowed with such a gift were regarded as 'cloth ears' and I know that I was one of them. Having sat at one time in an office in Manchester Square immediately above those of several 'tasters' below, I know that I was definitely not one of the 'golden ears' brigade.

The electronics side of EMI was a world apart from the Group's records and entertainment operations. Based at Hayes, near London Airport, its research centre and factories complex had a long history of brilliant innovation and high standards of technical excellence. Yet this side of EMI's work was almost unknown to most of the general public. The Hayes contribution to the development of radar in the Second World War, for example, was by no means fully appreciated outside specialist fields, any more than the creation of the world's first public TV system by its research scientists in 1936.

EMI was sometimes described as a 'one-off' company with a diversity of activities. It certainly never lacked interest to the outside world. There was news about it in the national press almost every day. The City was constantly interested, and not simply in terms of the share price alone. Financial analysts from leading firms of stockbrokers were frequently in touch, asking to come and see me or to talk over the telephone. They were usually well informed about EMI's business affairs, although I often spent long hours giving them background information on various aspects of the Group's activities. The best of them could size up, pretty accurately, how EMI was doing, without my disclosing anything confidential. Between us, I liked to think, there was a healthy mutual respect.

1971

The early months of 1971 were dominated by the impending departure of Bryan Forbes. He had been head of production at Elstree Film Studios since 1969 but had decided to leave. His time with EMI had not been a happy one.

I knew Bryan Forbes only slightly, although as a movie fan I had always admired the quality of his work as a film-maker. He was an outstanding scriptwriter – in the opinion of many in the business, one of the best in the world. He was a highly imaginative film director as well. His decision to leave EMI was sad in many ways, and it fell to me to issue a lengthy formal press announcement – the product of much drafting and re-drafting over a period of several weeks by lawyers. Shortly before I was due to do so on the appointed day, Bryan rang me to say that he felt the release should be issued earlier than the time originally agreed as the news of his departure was beginning to leak. It would probably leak even more, he said, after he had addressed Elstree's 500 employees later that morning.

He was, of course, right – and he knew that he was going to be right. I rushed the release out, but it proved largely a waste of time because the story was already hitting the mid-morning edition of the *Evening Standard*. The news not only headlined the front page but there was also a lavishly illustrated double-page feature about Bryan's career and his film-making inside the paper – written by Alexander Walker, the *Standard*'s influential film critic. It looked very good from Bryan's standpoint. I reminded myself that alongside his other gifts and skills, Bryan was an extremely able self-publicist.

A few months later news of an even more serious character broke around EMI's head. Capitol Industries, the company's US-based company and its most important subsidiary, suddenly plunged into heavy loss after many years of profit. It was a loss that could not be offset by improved results elsewhere in the Group and so there was no dividend paid that year to shareholders.

Although Capitol's rapid decline was partly due to a general drop in sales experienced by all the record companies in North America, the fact remained that Capitol had for too long enjoyed an easy profitability. The Beatles had provided massive success for year after year but their impact was now lessening. Capitol had not during this period signed any new artists of sufficient pulling power to offset the deteriorating position.

EMI took prompt remedial action. The president of Capitol was fired, together with a large number of the company's vice-presidents and 30 per cent of staff. New cost controls were put into effect and new management installed. Bhaskar Menon, a former head of EMI India and at the age of 34 one of the Group's most efficient record executives, was dispatched from London to Hollywood to take charge. He was strongly supported by John Read, who made frequent visits to California to help him restore Capitol's fortunes. Within two years Bhaskar not only succeeded in getting Capitol back into profitability but also laid the foundations for renewed prosperity. It was a remarkable management feat, and rapidly made him a leading figure in the world record industry.

1972

The extension of my PR activities for EMI continued throughout 1972. My small team by this time included a number of talented people: Alan Kaupe, who joined me from Thames TV, where he had been publicity manager; Rachel Nelson, also from Thames, a top press relations operator; Sue Coldstream, her able and charming assistant, excellent at organising events; John Lewis, a very knowledgeable American, my administrative right-hand who, together with my secretary Danny Spence, provided a most helpful and efficient personal back-up.

Some time later, when Alan Kaupe moved to the music side of EMI, I was joined by Peter Williams, a dogged ex-newspaperman and former colleague of mine from my steel industry days; and also by Colin Woodley, a brilliant young technical publicist from Hayes, where he had been electronics publicity manager.

We also expanded our international PR operations covering North America, Japan and mainland Europe, the Group's most important markets for recorded music and other products.

In North America our on-the-ground PR representation continued to be led by Gordon Molesworth, a veteran consultant based in New York. He concentrated on relations with the Wall Street financial community and press and his other activities included the preparation and issue (in collaboration with myself) of a regular EMI news bulletin to selected 'opinion formers' throughout the US.

Gordon had an interesting background. Aged around 60, white-haired and possessed of a rare brand of American courtesy, he was one of the relatively few people ever to meet and do business with Howard Hughes, the eccentric and highly reclusive inventor and multi-millionaire. It happened some years before I met Gordon, when he was working as head of PR and publicity for the US Atomic

Energy Authority. The Authority was in business negotiation with the Hughes Corporation at the time and as a result Gordon got to meet Howard Hughes himself in somewhat bizarre circumstances. One day he received a summons by telephone to meet Hughes in Hollywood, to travel there from New York and await further information on arrival. Gordon complied, only to find himself hanging about in Hollywood for a couple of days or so before finally getting another call – this time asking him to turn up at midnight at a house on the outskirts of town. When he did so, he found the house and its surroundings deserted, although a couple of the lights in the house itself were burning. The front door was unlocked, so he went inside and seated himself on one of two chairs in an otherwise unfurnished room. After sitting alone in this manner for several minutes, Howard Hughes quietly entered – wearing nothing but a pair of shorts and sneakers. 'His handshake was pretty off-putting, cold and clammy,' Gordon told me, 'but once he started talking about the engineering project he had in mind he livened up. He became talkative and very articulate. He was undoubtedly an outstanding engineer who knew exactly what he wanted. I felt afterwards, and I've always felt since, that it was something that most people never fully recognised.'

EMI's business interests in North America took me quite frequently to the US, mainly to New York and Hollywood. My first impression of Hollywood was one that never altered. I always thought it rather disappointing – the reverse of glamorous. It was flat, suburban-looking, with large and in some cases very curious-looking houses where film stars had once lived and were now occupied by wealthy doctors, dentists and lawyers. The most interesting-looking building in the whole place, I thought (and without prejudice) was Capitol's head office on Vine Street: a tallish, stout-looking round tower of a building with projecting sunblinds interleaved between its storeys, so that the entire structure resembled a giant pile of gramophone records. Once seen, never forgotten.

Back in the UK, as my PR activities continued to grow, John Read also asked me to 'look after' a small film production outfit specialising in the making and marketing of industrial and commercial films and not at that time attached to any particular part of EMI's mainstream operations. I took the job on, christening the outfit EMI Special Films Unit in the process.

The unit was headed by Richard Dunn, a strikingly handsome young man of British-Icelandic parentage who, after gaining a boxing blue at university, became a schoolteacher. He was a 'natural' for the film and TV industries, however – a talented scriptwriter and producer, and (as he later demonstrated) a most effective manager and business leader.

I was very happy to work with Richard. The unit produced some 20 films under his direction, including a series for the CBI which I helped him to obtain. Later he joined Thames TV and had an outstanding career there, becoming chief executive and gaining widespread public attention for the manner in which he successfully overcame a protracted trades union dispute – notably by getting his managers to run the daily TV programme service, unaided, after the unions had withdrawn their labour.

Tragically, Richard died suddenly in 1998, at the age of 54, of a suspected heart attack. He was a great loss to the TV industry, a man of widely admired abilities to whom, in the opinion of many, even greater prospects would have presented themselves had he lived.

1972 was also the year when, to the general surprise of many people outside EMI and not a few inside it, Gregory Peck joined the board of Capitol Records in Hollywood. 'All very well, but what does he know about the record business?' a woman reporter on the *Financial Times* asked me rather sniffily.

Capitol, of course, took an entirely different view. 'He brings a sensitivity to the performing areas of the industry, at board level, which Capitol is very fortunate and honoured to have,' their official press release said.

Shortly afterwards, Peck flew into London and had lunch with John Read and several other EMI executives – including me. Although I had greatly admired his performances in many of his films (all of which I had seen) I found him a rather reserved, wooden character. Imposing, well-built and handsome, he was dressed conservatively, like a banker, and he behaved like one. Our conversation throughout lunch was of the most dignified kind, hardly touching upon film industry matters. Peck did mention at the coffee stage, however, that he had a project in mind: he wanted to make a film called *The Dove*, telling the true-life story of a boy's single-handed yachting adventures sailing around the world, with the various dangers and privations the boy had encountered across the oceans.

After lunch, Peck was mobbed in the lobby of EMI's Manchester Square offices by many of the girls who worked there. Word had speedily got round that he was in the building, and they all wanted to see him in the flesh and, if possible, get his autograph. He charmed every one of them, smiling and talking as he signed the books of all those who got near him.

We had a slight difficulty after that, however. There was no transport immediately available to take Peck to his tailor in Savile Row and then on to London Airport, which was where he wanted to go. As a result, my own smallish Rover 2000 plus a temporary driver were hurriedly summoned from the basement garage below. With some difficulty we helped Peck manoeuvre his large frame into the back seat. 'Are you comfortable, Mr Peck?' I asked.

'I guess I'll manage OK,' he said, and the car drove off.

Eighteen months later *The Dove*, produced by Gregory Peck, with EMI backing, was premiered in London. Although well produced, with a strong storyline, it did not seem to appeal to the public and was not a success. I wondered why Peck should have bothered with it at all, and I was not the only one.

Meanwhile a further major film was premiered in London during the year, this time under the MGM-EMI banner. *Lady Caroline Lamb* starred Sarah Miles as the wild Lady C and Richard Chamberlain as the poet Lord Byron. Cameo roles were played by several big-name actors, including Ralph Richardson as George III and Laurence Olivier as the Duke of Wellington. The film was not really the success that was hoped for, however.

Helen (my wife) and I attended the *Lady Caroline* premiere. It was one of a dozen or so that we went to over the next few years. The pattern, sadly, was always much the same. Black tie and evening dress. Complimentary tickets for film industry VIPs and their guests, with everyone else paying hefty prices for their programmes and seats (net proceeds going to the charity the premiere was being given in aid of). Royalty attending as patrons of the charity (good publicity value, it was always hoped) plus stars if available and a host of film industry business people. Red carpet treatment all round, with photographers taking pictures of anyone of note in sight. Cinema foyer cleared except for 'receiving line' of film industry notables greeting Royalty on their arrival. Everyone in the auditorium rising when Royalty entered a few minutes later, saluted by a fanfare from state trumpeters standing on the stage. Royalty then took their seats. Lights went down and the film began.

It was always a matter of considerable puzzlement to me why film premieres were always so similar – why fresh and original ideas were never tried out. Perhaps it was not

possible – I didn't really know, and organising premieres
was thankfully not within my remit anyway. Nevertheless, I
often felt that the film industry didn't really care for change,
despite all the clamour and razzmatazz surrounding it. Not
where premieres were concerned, at any rate.

1973

The year 1973 was a very special one for EMI. It marked
the 75th anniversary of the company's worldwide
involvement in the recorded music business – an
involvement that stretched back to the beginning of the
20th century, when the great tenor Caruso was among the
first of the thousands of major artists recorded by the
company in subsequent years.

To mark the anniversary, EMI held a special concert at
the Royal Festival Hall. It was a prestigious occasion.
Under the batons of Sir Adrian Boult and Andre Previn,
the London Symphony Orchestra performed a wide-
ranging programme of works by Elgar, Mozart, Bruch,
Franz Lehar and William Walton, who also wrote a special
fanfare for the occasion. Annaliese Rothenberger, Nicolai
Gedda and Yehudi Menuhin were the soloists for the Lehar
and Bruch pieces.

The concert was devised by my colleague Peter Andry,
head of EMI's classical recording division. My own job was
largely administrative – supervising the front-of-house
arrangements, seating and so on, and above all making sure
that all was well with the VIP's, of whom there were many.

Some 500 people attended the concert. The VIPs
included ambassadors, political leaders (the Prime Minister,
Edward Heath, was among them) and distinguished figures
in the world of international music. Maria Callas was there.
She sat in the Royal Box with Sir Joseph Lockwood.
Tactfully she remarked to him: 'EMI is the only record

company that pays my royalties promptly.' (Callas had strong links with EMI, not only as a major artist, but also because several people on the company's classical recording side were personal friends. In the final years of her life, when she was a lonely woman living in a flat in Paris, she used to telephone one or other of them every day, simply to talk to someone, so it was said.)

All EMI's guests at the concert were in evening dress – possibly to the surprise of the rest of the audience, who were not. The idea behind this was, as well as marking the special occasion, the guests would be easily identifiable for the supper party afterwards, to be held in the nearby Festival Hall restaurant, and thereby prevent gate-crashing. Security was also an important issue as the Prime Minister was attending. Before the performance started there was a complete search of the building by police with dogs. The large windows near his supper party were heavily sandbagged on the outside as well.

1973 was also a year of other newsworthy happenings. The New London Theatre, built on the site of the old Winter Garden Theatre in Drury Lane, was officially opened under EMI management. A number of 'famous name' actors were present, Alec Guinness and Trevor Howard among them. All the men marched up and down the new stage, stamping their feet upon the boards now and then, and also standing stock still every so often, gazing out at the darkened auditorium from fixed positions. They were testing things out, I suppose, although none of the ladies present copied them, Cicely Courtneidge looking faintly puzzled, I thought.

The New London really was a new type of theatre; a 900-seater incorporating the latest technology that enabled the conventional auditorium to be transformed into an amphitheatre at the throw of a switch. It was not a successful theatre to begin with, however. The first productions mounted – a play featuring Peter Ustinov, followed by the pop musical *Grease* – had disappointing runs, and for several years the building was used as a TV studio. (It was not until 1981, in fact, when Andrew Lloyd Webber's musical *Cats* opened, that everything took off. *Cats* ran until 2012, up to that time the longest running musical in West End history.)

Although 1973 had been a special one for EMI it was nevertheless the year that, for everybody, ended on a gloomy note. A worrying national crisis had been brought about by the Heath government's confrontation with the miners over a pay dispute, culminating in the country being put on a three-day working week. Within companies generally, including EMI, frequent crisis meetings became the order of the day.

I attended all the EMI meetings, held in the boardroom in Manchester Square. At the conclusion of one of them I left the meeting together with one of our non-executive directors whom I knew to be a very wealthy man. As we walked towards the lift he said to me quietly: 'Worrying business. My shares have gone down frightfully, about 150 thou. I suppose you're having a bad time, too. How are you placed?'

'I wouldn't care to put a figure on it,' I replied. (I owned no shares of any kind. I had no money to put anywhere, actually.)

1974

Another aspect of my job in which I found myself regularly involved was the drafting of citations for honours and awards. Twice a year, for birthday and New Year honours, we were asked by the Department of Trade and Industry to submit citations, signed off by the chairman, detailing the careers and achievements of suitable EMI candidates for CBE, OBE, MBE and BEM. For this purpose a small number of application forms were supplied by the DTI, together with guidance on how to complete them. Even so, the writing of citations took a good deal of time, especially with the discreet background research involved, and several years might elapse before an honour or award was announced, if ever.

I came to realise very quickly that whatever the merits of candidates in leading companies such as EMI, there were probably hundreds of other deserving people who never had the benefit of having their names put forward for them, simply because they were not linked to any sort of system. And the well-established system that existed for parts of industry itself was basically unfair. For a start, the DTI issued application forms only to companies on its list, but this list did *not* include any company engaged in military work. The latter (and there were far fewer of them) were all part of a separate system operated by the Ministry of Defence. On a simple arithmetical basis, therefore, anyone on the MOD 'net' stood a far higher chance of securing an honour than those on any DTI list. (Years later, after leaving EMI, *The Times* published a letter from me suggesting that the 'systems' should be widened to include other sections of society, notably the volunteer sector, and that there should also be opportunities for individual members of the public to be formally nominated. My letter may or may not have had any effect, but changes have since been made.)

1974 proved heavier than usual for EMI social functions. The year marked Sir Joseph Lockwood's 70th birthday, and on that day he duly stepped down from the chairmanship of the company after 20 years in office. John Read, his successor, held a surprise dinner for him at Quaglino's, which I helped to arrange. Over 100 people attended, including Whitehall mandarins, captains of industry and other business leaders, together with several recording stars. The cabaret included children from the Royal Ballet School who danced in his honour (he had helped the school for many years), and also Vera Lynn. She sang some of the wartime and other songs she had made so famous, persuading with some difficulty her rather stuffy middle-aged audience to join in.

We also had the premiere of one of EMI's most successful films that year – *Murder on the Orient Express*, Agatha Christie's best-selling thriller. The premiere was held at the ABC Cinema in Shaftsbury Avenue in aid of the NSPCC and other charities. It was attended by the Queen, the Duke of Edinburgh, Princess Anne and Captain Mark Phillips. A host of other VIP's and stars, including Earl Mountbatten, Ingrid Bergman and David Niven were also present.

The supper party at Claridges afterwards was equally glamorous. Many of the stars of the film were there – Albert Finney, John Gielgud, Wendy Hiller, Lauren Bacall – as indeed was Agatha Christie, who rarely appeared in public. White-haired and elderly, she left the party early, carefully wheeled out of the Claridges ballroom by Mountbatten. Everybody rose to clap her as she departed. It was possibly her last public appearance, for she died a year or so later.

Helen and I managed to have a few words with Mountbatten during the party – Helen having served on his staff at Combined Operations headquarters in London during the war, and I myself having been one of his many soldiers. 'I always picked the prettiest Wrens to work for me,' said Mountbatten smilingly as he chatted to my wife.

'I'd still follow that man anywhere,' Helen said to me as she walked away afterwards.

EMI's film premieres were organised by David Jones, as were the supper parties afterwards, although I used to help him with the latter. David was the veteran publicity director of EMI Films. His wife Ettie worked with him as his secretary and had done so for 40 years – a unique partnership. The two of them had first met as teenagers, working together in the old Wardour Street offices at RKO Radio. I once asked David if he could remember the name of the very first star he had ever had dealings with. 'Helen Twelvetrees,' he said (and that was going back a long way: she was a Hollywood star in the 1930s).

A star of a different kind whom I got to know well was Joe Loss. He was also a veteran, but in the world of dance bands – not films. He had been a recording artist under contract to EMI since 1931, one of the longest-serving on the roster. His dance bands were celebrated (he ran more than one) and he was always in demand at high society functions – and at Buckingham Palace, too. He played for us every year at EMI's annual Christmas party. 'If I can't get everyone on the dance floor to enjoy themselves,' he used to say to me, 'I've failed.'

We held an unusual reception in 1974 for one of our most famous overseas artists, Lata Mangeshkar of India. Affectionately known as 'The Nightingale of Bollywood' and credited in the *Guinness Book of Records* with having made more recordings than anyone else in the world (over 30,000, in fact) her haunting voice and music drew large crowds of Indians and Europeans to the concert that she gave at the Royal Albert Hall. At the press reception that we held for her afterwards she was presented by EMI with the customary gold disc – in reality, as was always the case, a gold-lacquered LP. Unfortunately, when she returned to India there was trouble with the Customs officials at the airport: they seemed to think she was attempting to smuggle real gold into the country, and apparently it took a good deal of bureaucratic hassling before she was finally allowed through.

When I was once visiting Elstree Studios I met Vincent Price, who was starring in a horror film being made there. He stood with me at the side of the set as we talked, waiting to be called for the next take. He was wearing sinister make-up and an all-enveloping black cloak. 'What a lark it all is,' he drawled, puffing at a cigarette. 'I'm much more interested in cooking and paintings, really.' (He was, in fact, highly knowledgeable about both subjects, as most people know.)

That particular visit to Elstree was memorable for me for one other reason: built sets in studios were beginning to decline in number. Films were being shot increasingly on location whenever possible, to cut costs and achieve maximum realism. In Elstree's case the effect was to start reducing the 500-strong staff, most of them highly-skilled craftsmen, by 90 per cent. Elstree became, in fact, a 'four-wall' studio, its premises open to independent producers to rent and use for their own productions – including dubbing and other post-production work.

I had always enjoyed walking round vacant film sets in studios whenever possible – to see how they were built and to admire the craftsmanship that invariably went into the making of them. This went back to the late 1930s, when I was one of a party of boys selected by MGM from our school at Bushey, near Watford, to work as a 'schoolboy extra' in the film *Goodbye, Mr Chips*, starring Robert Donat and Greer Garson, then being shot at Denham Studios a few miles away. The main set at Denham was the school quadrangle and surrounding buildings that featured in the film's story and where many of the crowd scenes in which we all took part were shot. The realism of the set, down to the smallest detail, fascinated me – as did a vast exterior set constructed on the back lot of the studio for another film, *The Thief of Baghdad*, for which filming had started at Denham but (owing to the outbreak of war) was later finished in Hollywood.

Years later, working for EMI, I saw some of the scenes being shot at Elstree for *Murder on the Orient Express*. Much of the film's action takes place in a railway carriage, and for this purpose technicians had sawn an old, disused Orient Express carriage in half to enable access for the camera crew. They then refurbished the two sections of the carriage to restore its authentic 1930s look.

Some time later I also had the chance to walk over a 'moonscape' set at Elstree, built for the first *Star Wars* film. This was a miracle of contrivance by the set-builders: 'missiles', half-buried in the ground, had been fashioned (when one looked very closely) from bits of old cars, washing machines and goodness knows what else – all most cleverly done and barely detectable.

1975

After working with Cliff Michelmore for five years on the development of EMI Audio Visual Services, the video cassette company that they had started together in 1970, Gordon Reece began a surprising new assignment that took him out of EMI.

A strong and dedicated member of the Conservative Party, he was close to Margaret Thatcher who made him her media adviser in 1975 – working from Conservative Central Office. For this purpose he was officially seconded from EMI for two years, and it was arranged that his expenses were to be split 50/50 between Central Office and ourselves during this period.

John Read asked me to 'look after' Gordon so far as EMI were concerned. 'Looking after' Gordon proved to be largely a question of signing off EMI's share of his expenses. These arrived at regular intervals, every few weeks or so, and invariably totalled two or three hundred pounds – mainly for champagne and cigars. I signed the bills, usually without query, although I did write to Gordon for more detail on one occasion. His expenses, of course, later became a matter of raised eyebrows within Central Office itself – so much so that Lord McAlpine, the party's treasurer, once had to explain to Baroness Young, the party's deputy chairman: 'Gordon is a Rolls-Royce among publicists, and he only runs on champagne.'

However costly he may have been, Gordon proved more than worth it to Margaret Thatcher and the Tory Party. For a start, as an experienced TV producer he knew how to improve her television appearance. He influenced changes in her hair style and her manner of speaking – reportedly seeking the advice of a voice coach from the National Theatre for the latter purpose. Later he became director of publicity at Central Office and played a significant behind-the-scenes role in the 1979 general election. He also advised at the 1983 and 1987 elections and finally received a knighthood. He idolised Margaret Thatcher and she, in turn, staunchly supported him as 'one of us'.

The year 1975 was strongly dominated by the increasing success and fast-moving expansion of EMI's medical business – arising from the pioneering invention, several years before, of diagnostic brain scanners by Godfrey Hounsfield, an EMI research scientist.

Godfrey conceived the idea of harnessing computers to X-rays, a highly innovative concept that gave birth to a new branch of medical science – computerised axial tomography, or CAT for short. In 1972, following the announcement of his invention, the EMI-Scanner for brain disease examination and diagnosis was successfully launched by presentations to large audiences of radiologists in Britain and America. By 1975 further technical development of the Scanner enabled its diagnostic capabilities to be extended to the whole body. We announced this news to the world by releasing a number of pictures, taken under laboratory conditions and first presented by Godfrey to a symposium of doctors at a major international conference in Bermuda. They clearly showed the success of the whole-body trials.

Although it is always dangerous to describe any form of innovation in medical science as a breakthrough, these pictures truly were – and their reception by the medical profession and the press was little short of sensational. *The Times* in London ran a front-page story, complete with picture, emphasising the importance of the news, and the world's press rapidly took their cue accordingly. Over ensuing weeks and months we had difficulty, at times, in coping with the flood of enquiries and requests for special interviews with Godfrey Hounsfield and his colleagues. In publicity terms, we had almost a runaway situation on our hands. The City became excited as well – probably far too excited to begin with, at least in some cases, when rather wild predictions of the effect the new Scanner would have on EMI's future profits would prove, in the long run, both euphoric and misleading – despite continuing efforts on our part to keep the news in perspective and to relate it in conservative terms.

As worldwide interest in the Scanner rapidly grew, so did interest on the part of various VIPs, among them the Duke of Edinburgh. He paid a special visit to the Hayes factory during the year and saw how the Scanners were being made. He was sharp and bright as usual, asking well-informed questions and taking a close personal interest in the work being done.

Another distinguished visitor was Sir Nicholas ('Nicko') Henderson, who was on the point of becoming the British Ambassador to France. A professional diplomat, he had set himself the task of visiting leading UK companies before taking up his post in Paris. His interest in EMI was, of course, the Scanner. I took him to Hayes and spent the entire day with him, taking him round the factory and the EMI research centre where Godfrey and his colleagues worked. We were all most impressed by his incisive questioning and by his rapid assimilation of any information he asked for.

1976

With EMI reporting a continuance of good progress on all fronts in the financial year 1975/76 our corporate PR was riding high. It is axiomatic, of course, that a company's public relations are invariably as good, or as bad, as its performance. When financial results are good, the company's image is brightly burnished. When results are bad, the image suffers accordingly and can only be improved by restoring good performance. There are times, however, when a company walks into problems not entirely of its own making that can never be fully defended.

One such problem – probably the most difficult of its kind in EMI's history – arose in October 1976 through the signing of the Sex Pistols. This group, four young men, all Londoners, was signed by EMI Records in response to the growing 'punk music wave' then emerging. The Sex Pistols was a group destined to last less than three years and produce only four singles and one album, yet its influence was profound. What really offended many members of the British public, however, was the Pistols' calculated offensiveness as part of its act. Raucous and riotous behaviour was the order of the day – plenty of four-letter swearing and gestures, spitting, violence (smashing up furniture in public places in at least one instance).

The group's behaviour first became an issue for EMI when they took part in an evening programme interview on Thames TV with presenter Bill Grundy. They apparently took an immediate dislike to each other, with the Sex Pistols ultimately swearing vigorously and offensively and encouraged to do so by Grundy (for which he was later suspended). The public reaction to all this was highly adverse, to say the least. Thames TV received hundreds of telephone calls, and there were a great number of complaints to the national press by outraged viewers. I myself received a barrage of calls from Fleet Street journalists at my home later that evening, and was asked to comment on behalf of EMI. I had not seen the show, and I could only indicate that the Sex Pistols incident was seemingly disgraceful and that EMI would be looking into the matter immediately. The following morning the press was full of angry comments about the TV show – totally condemning the Sex Pistols' conduct (in one newspaper under a large-type front-page headline 'The Filth and the Fury'). EMI suddenly had a very sizeable PR problem on its hands.

Within the company there was, perhaps inevitably, a strong division of opinion about the Sex Pistols. Pop music executives, keen to cash in on the significance of the new 'wave', upheld the Pistols' signing. Corporate executives at EMI's head office (including me), who were not directly concerned with the record business, were worried about the impact that the Pistols' behaviour would make on EMI's interests elsewhere – with government, for example, where EMI had important ongoing relations with various Ministries – notably Health and Defence. John Read himself, as EMI's chairman, was already receiving phone calls from aggrieved shareholders, urging him to take rapid corrective action and to sack the Sex Pistols out of hand.

The controversy raged for several weeks. So much so, that Read finally took the unprecedented step of making a special policy statement (which I drafted for him) at EMI's annual general meeting in December. This statement said in part:

'Throughout its history as a recording company, EMI has sought to behave within contemporary limits of decency and good taste – taking into account not only the rigid conventions of one section of society, but also the increasingly liberal attitudes of other (perhaps larger) sections of society at any given time.

'Today, there is in EMI's experience not only an overwhelming sense of permissiveness – as demonstrated by the content of books, newspapers and magazines, as well as records and films – but also a good deal of questioning by various sections of society both young and old, eg. What is decent or in good taste compared to the attitudes of, say, 20 or 10 years ago?

'It is against this present-day social background that EMI has to make value judgements about the content of records in particular... Who is to decide what is objectionable or unobjectionable to the public at large today? When anyone sits down to consider this problem seriously, it will be found that there are widely differing attitudes between people of all ages and all walks of life as to what can be shown or spoken or sung.

'Our view within EMI is that we should seek to discourage records that are likely to give offence to the majority of people. In this context, changing public attitudes have to be taken into account. EMI should not set itself up as a public censor, but it does seek to encourage restraint.'

Shortly after the company's AGM, because of increasingly bad public behaviour by the Sex Pistols – notably at London Airport – EMI's contract with the group was terminated at a cost of £40,000. The Sex Pistols were then signed by two other record companies, one after the other, both of them encountering similar behaviour difficulties and public protests. Eventually the entire Sex Pistols story petered out pathetically – and tragically. Whilst on tour in the United States the group broke up and one of its members committed suicide.

Some weeks after the termination of the Sex Pistols' contract John Read asked me to organise a high-level in-house conference of a highly unusual nature. We arranged for 40 people, all involved in or connected with EMI's business affairs, to sit round a table behind closed doors in a nearby hotel in order to review and discuss contemporary permissiveness – and in particular the public's increasingly relaxed attitudes towards it. Those taking part included main board directors and their wives, and senior executives from the company's music, films, TV, and entertainment businesses.

To set the scene, I arranged for a 20-minute introductory video to be made. Shot by an EMI video team walking around London's streets and filming the public at random, it was designed to show how times had changed – how easy it was for anyone, children included, to access pornographic magazines, films or other obscene material in newsagents, record shops, cinemas, book stores and elsewhere. The question was: how could EMI deal with this on its own, bearing in mind that any material it refused to handle, such as an offensive recording, could find a home with a competitor company and probably achieve high sales through its notoriety if nothing else? (As had happened, albeit for a very short period, in the case of the Sex Pistols.)

There was no clear-cut answer to the problem, and of course there still isn't, but at least the video focused attention upon it and stimulated a vigorous discussion. Somewhat surprisingly, at any rate to me, the majority of those present – middle-aged people for the most part, representing a more conservative generation – were far more concerned with violence in films, on TV and in the media generally than with sexual obscenity. No definite conclusions were reached by the end of the discussion, or new plans for EMI action made. But perhaps a seed had been sown; and in the meantime, looking back at the signing of the Sex Pistols, for EMI it had undoubtedly proved a signing too far.

Less controversial and more successful events had taken place earlier in the year. The most important was a large-scale national conference, held in London, which brought together 100 of EMI's top executives from across the world for a series of review meetings. The talks, discussions and presentations took place over five days, and a final dinner was held which was attended by the Prime Minister, Harold Wilson. He was in sparkling form and plainly in a mood to entertain his hosts and their guests. He paid EMI a lot of compliments, reinforcing his comments by reading from favourable press comment that had recently appeared in the newspapers (at that time, good stories about EMI were appearing in the national press almost daily, mainly on the City pages). Like a conjurer doing a music-hall turn, he produced a stream of press clippings from his jacket and trouser pockets, one after the other, and read them out in his rather sonorous, gritty style. He got a lot of laughter and a big clap at the end of it all. He was a very good performer, a master politician of course. It made the day for all of us, certainly myself, as the conference took considerable organising.

Around the same time EMI held a special reception in London to mark Yehudi Menuhin's 45 years as a classical recording artist for the company. It was also his 60th birthday. It seemed extraordinary (and indeed it was) that this small, slightly built man had actually started to record for EMI at the age of 15 in 1931, playing the violin as a soloist with an orchestra under the baton of Sir Edward Elgar at Abbey Road. We presented him with a life-size bronze bust of himself, sculpted by one of our own classical music executives, Austin Bennett. Among those present was Krishna Menon, an uncle of our own Bhaskar Menon (head of EMI's music business in North America) who had flown into London for the occasion. As a young reporter, I had covered Krishna Menon's time shortly after the war when he was India's High Commissioner in London. His speeches always commanded widespread attention.

We also had a major film premiere that year. *Aces High* was a dramatic, moving film about young fighter pilots serving on the Western Front during the First World War. Many of them did not survive, their average life being about seven days after first going into action. The film brought about a vivid personal memory of my stepfather, who flew on the Western Front as a young observer/gunner in the Royal Flying Corps at the age of just 18. He survived the war, fortunately, and was awarded a DFC for his bravery. He rarely talked of his experiences, and I often used to wonder how he or any of his comrades ever managed to summon the courage to fly in the flimsy-looking aircraft of WWI – let alone fight in them.

Throughout 1976 Godfrey Hounsfield's revolutionary medical diagnostic EMI-Scanner went from strength to strength – winning more and more orders overseas, especially in the USA. Their use was also growing in British hospitals, often purchased as a result of local fund-raising efforts (the cost of a Scanner was around £1 million) as well as the generosity of private donors.

One such purchase, thanks to a private donor, was by the Royal Sussex Hospital in Brighton. Earl Mountbatten was asked by the hospital to help 'launch' the new Scanner by undertaking an official opening ceremony and thereby gain useful publicity for it as a new regional facility. He did so with his usual straightforward charm and efficiency. Afterwards I found myself talking to him and, perhaps inevitably, the conversation turned to wartime service. I told him that I had been one of his young officers in the Commandos. 'Ah, yes,' he said. 'You chaps always meant a great deal to me. Mind you, I used to have to spend a fair amount of time telling everybody that you weren't jailbirds.' He was referring to an oft-repeated wartime rumour that the Commandos had all been recruited from prisons. I never came across any jailbirds myself, although there were reportedly one or two professional safe-breakers and other ex-criminal specialists somewhere in our ranks – no doubt recruited, like the rest of us, for what was termed in those days 'special service of a hazardous nature'.

1977

Two nagging 'moral maze' issues confronted EMI with increasing insistence in 1977.

The first was continuing pressure by activists to persuade selected companies – EMI was their first choice – to withdraw from all types of military business. This group, known as The Campaign Against the Arms Trade (CAAT), was a combination of Christian and Pacifist organisations, notably Pax Christi and the Quakers plus CND and *Peace News*. The CAAT's argument, pursued in various ways, including face-to-face discussions with John Read and myself, was that EMI could well afford to withdraw from the manufacture of military products (emotively termed 'arms', although the equipment we made was essentially defensive, mainly radar) because of our profitable music and entertainments businesses. We prevailed with our own arguments against CAAT's, namely that our military production, under rigid contract to HM Government, was non-aggressive. Eventually the CAAT trailed away to pursue other quarries.

The second 'moral maze' issue concerned the level of wages paid in South Africa to black workers in companies owned by British interests. This matter had first been raised by the journalist Adam Raphael, writing in the *Guardian* newspaper in 1973. In a series of articles he named a large number of UK companies (EMI was not included to begin with) whose South African subsidiaries, according to his researches, were paying wages to their African employees below the so-called 'Poverty Datum Line' (PDL).

The PDL had been established by a leading South African university as a result of its own social research work. EMI was one of the British companies named in Raphael's later lists because it had recently acquired a small security company in Cape Town that employed 400 Africans as guards and watchmen – available on hire to local firms for basic security patrol work by day and night. The principal EMI business in South Africa, long established, was based in Johannesburg where it owned and operated a record-pressing factory. The wages paid to EMI's black employees in Johannesburg was well above the PDL but those in Cape Town were not. Raphael therefore definitely had a point in the latter respect.

The problem with the Cape Town company, however, was that it had three local competitors, all South African firms, who would not agree to a general raising of wage levels for all black employees, despite repeated proposals to that effect by EMI. In the end we (EMI) decided to sell our

Cape Town company – and here was another irony – the only taker being another, smaller, British firm that was not particularly well known and therefore not under the spotlight.

Following Adam Raphael's articles in the *Guardian*, and before the sale of the Cape Town company took place, my deputy, Peter Williams, spent three weeks in Johannesburg and Cape Town compiling a personal report for John Read. Peter was himself a former newspaperman with a tenacious ability to dig out facts. He came back and delivered a report that provided an independent and fully up-to-date assessment of EMI's personnel policies and wage levels in all its South African businesses. His enquiries took him, among other places, into the Soweto township outside Johannesburg where most of the company's black employees lived. He was told, at the time, that he was one of the few Europeans ever to have been there.

Aside from these 'moral maze' problems, EMI continued to make further progress: the results for the financial year 1976/77 were in fact the highest achieved in the company's history. Sales of the EMI-Scanner again contributed substantially to the results, although there were signs in the US, the largest market, that all was not well. There was a mounting desire on the part of the US authorities to cut the costs of healthcare, including expenditure on imported medical equipment. This did not bode well for the Scanner's future.

Meanwhile, for the music world, 1977 marked the 100th anniversary of the invention of recorded sound. Back in 1877 Thomas Edison had produced his 'tinfoil' phonograph, and this had been followed ten years later by Emile Berliner's 'flat disc' gramophone.

EMI celebrated the anniversary by holding a Gala Concert at the Royal Festival Hall, featuring the London

Philharmonic Orchestra under three distinguished conductors – Paavo Berglund, Willi Boskovsky and Maxim Shostakovitch (son of Dimitri).

The concert reflected EMI's vast international range of recorded music experience, including (as it did) works by Sibelius, Mozart, Johann Strauss II and Tchaikovsky. It was once again organised by my colleague Peter Andry, head of the classical records division, whilst my own part was to supervise seating and the handling of VIP guests. Proceeds from the concert went to an important cause – helping to fund a new rehearsal hall in Southwark, to be called the Henry Wood rehearsal hall, which would provide a base for the two great London orchestras – the LSO and the London Philharmonic – which they had hitherto lacked.

The centenary of the invention of recorded sound was also marked in a further and hopefully imaginative way. For many years EMI had maintained on its Hayes site a small collection of historic gramophones manufactured by EMI itself and by rival companies, the earliest dating back to 1878. To this was added an important Dutch collection, known as the Bleeker collection, which EMI had acquired in 1974. After discussion within the company I asked the Science Museum in London if they would like to exhibit these machines to mark the centenary, and they expressed keen interest. Various EMI colleagues and outside experts then put everything together. The resultant exhibition, opened by Dame Janet Baker, proved a great success and drew large numbers of visitors.

A commemorative event in yet another area of EMI's business also took place in 1977. Together with other company representatives I attended the unveiling of a Greater London Council 'blue plaque' at the former Ealing home of Alan Blumlein.

Blumlein was an EMI research engineer of undoubted genius. He worked for the company (and his country) during the 1930s and 40s, helping to develop various important technologies in the fields of telephone engineering, recorded sound, and TV picture transmission. He held 128 patents arising from his work, one of the most important being his 'binaural sound' system which he patented in 1931 (fully recognised by the record industry when LP stereo records were launched in 1951). In the mid-1930s he also developed electrical circuitry for an electronic method of picture transmission for TV: he later headed the EMI team that convinced the BBC in 1937 that it would be better to opt for that system rather than a mechanical one.

During the Second World War Blumlein concentrated upon sound detection systems for the tracking of aircraft (i.e. radar). He brought EMI into radar research by helping to develop airborne interception systems that could detect aircraft by night and also targets from the air regardless of weather conditions. In 1942, whilst testing a system in flight over England under conditions of great secrecy, he and other members of the team involved were tragically killed when the aircraft crashed in the West Country. He was 39 years of age when this happened.

It struck me as most extraordinarily dilatory, as I stood in the front garden of Blumlein's former home that June morning in 1977, that it had taken the GLC (and the London County Council before it) a full 35 years to recognise the immense importance of the contributions made to our country by Alan Dower Blumlein, Londoner.

Year Thirty: 1978

This was the year when EMI's fortunes began to decline seriously. There was a swift worldwide downturn in the music business and this affected the entire record industry, EMI included. In addition, the company's EMI-Scanner business experienced continuing competitive pressure internationally, particularly in the USA, its principal market, where US Government moves to cut healthcare costs further exacerbated the situation. Within two years, although few of us fully realised it at the time, EMI would undergo profound change.

Meanwhile there were a few bright moments, one of them being an occasion to mark the extremely long service to EMI of Len Wood, main board director and for many years head of EMI's music business affairs. By 1978 he had completed 50 years with EMI, having first started as a salesman with Columbia Graphophone (a predecessor company) in 1928.

Len, I found, was virtually a walking encyclopaedia of the music business. He knew everything about it, especially EMI's involvement, and always had the details of major artists' contracts at his fingertips – most notably EMI's contract with The Beatles, which he kept in a locked safe in his office. 'You'll have heard many stories of how The Beatles first came to be signed by EMI,' he was fond of saying. 'Let me tell you mine.' (His version, which was the accurate one, has also been often told. George Martin, one of his four staff producers at the time, was of course the man who first signed them up.)

As well as knowing countless artists, Len also knew their agents and managers even better. He was a dogged negotiator, and had to deal with a good many unpleasant people in the process. One of the most notorious was Don Arden, a veteran rock music manager who rejoiced in his fierce, intimidating reputation – he was called, among other names, the Al Capone of Pop. 'He always came into my office carrying a gun, and he usually placed it on the desk in front of me when he started to talk business,' Len once told me.

In 1978 Len was awarded a CBE in the New Year Honours list. It was well deserved. For many years he had served at the head of various music industry bodies, as well as working full-time for EMI. As in other cases, I wondered why it had taken so long for him to be recognised. I had drafted his original citation for the honour in 1975 (without his knowledge, of course) and it had taken three further submissions to the Honours authorities for the citation finally to 'ring the bell'.

Towards the end of the year we embarked on a major PR commitment, arising from the successful development of the EMI-Scanner since the early 1970s. At the invitation of the Institute of Electrical Engineers (as it then was) we undertook the task of mounting and delivering – at selected centres throughout Britain – the Institute's 50th annual Faraday Lecture. The choice of subject was left to EMI.

It was a large-scale operation, involving a team of six lecturers working on a rotational basis, supported by a small army of organisers and helpers. The lecturing team was led by Dr John Powell, the main board director in charge of EMI's medical electronics business. The support staff was headed by Colin Woodley and Clive Oates of my PR team.

Entitled 'The Diagnostic Electron' the whole travelling show, complete with a mass of audio-visual equipment, toured the country. The lecture was delivered 40 times in

15 cities and attended by a total of 60,000 members of the public, including schoolchildren. The entire operation lasted six months, finally completing in the spring of 1979.

1979

And so when 1979 dawned we were still busy with the Faraday Lecture tour. But this was against the background of a further decline in EMI's fortunes, and as the months went by there was increasing press talk of a possible take-over bid for the company. Despite rumours of many potential bidders, there was in fact only one definite offer. This came towards the end of the year from Thorn Electrical Industries and was accepted by EMI's shareholders. By the turn of the year a new company, Thorn EMI, had been created.

I was invited to stay on and become the company's first PR director, but I declined. I had been very happy at EMI but I had already decided to move on and work on my own; among other things I wanted to devote more time to writing, and to write a book. My PR team and other EMI friends gave me a heart-warming send-off, presenting me with a framed EMI gold disc inscribed 'For service beyond the call of duty'. I was very proud of that, and very proud of my team, several of whom remained my friends and have kept in touch with me to this day.

Looking back over the 30 years that I spent in corporate PR work for five companies, years that encompassed unexpected adventures in various parts of the world as well as major industrial and business developments in the UK, my greatest source of pride is that I was enabled to lead the PR and publicity team that helped to make known one of the greatest medical inventions of the last century, namely the EMI-Scanner. Much of the work was undertaken by Colin Woodley, but everyone in my team played a useful part. My own profile of the quiet, modest inventor, Sir Godfrey Hounsfield, EMI research scientist and Nobel prize-winner, was first published some years ago and forms, at any rate for me, a fitting Appendix to this book.

Today the PR business, in organisational terms, is very different to the one that I first entered in 1948. It has become a vast affair, offering dazzling careers and high rewards (even fortunes, in some cases) to those who now choose to take it up. PR has become more of a recognised profession, too, with at least 20 UK universities offering degree courses of one kind or another.

Yet whatever the merits of academic study might be, the fact remains that PR is essentially a matter of 'on the ground' practical capability. As well as being able to write, speak, and in all other ways communicate effectively, you need to be able to handle people with understanding, to reflect their needs and views in your actions, and above all to try always to anticipate, intelligently, the likely public consequences of private decision-making.

I greatly enjoyed, for the most part, my 30 years in corporate PR, meeting and working with hundreds of people in widely differing walks of life – steelworkers, car-makers, bridge builders, research scientists, electronics boffins, pop stars, and even film stars. People tell me that my wide-ranging career could not possibly be replicated in the world we now live in. If such is the case, and I believe it to be so, then I was truly a most fortunate PR pioneer.

* * * * * * * *

Appendix

SIR GODFREY HOUNSFIELD (1919–2004)

Creator of a Medical Marvel

Godfrey Hounsfield was the man responsible for one of the twentieth century's greatest medical breakthroughs – the invention of CAT scanners. Yet he was not medically trained, he never attended university, and he had only what many would regard as a limited scientific education.

Godfrey came of farming stock. He was born in 1919 on a Nottinghamshire farm and, as he later put it, enjoyed the freedom of an isolated country life. He was the youngest of five children, a quiet, solitary boy who was usually left by his brothers and sisters to follow his own inclinations. Gadgets of every kind, both electrical and mechanical, intrigued him from an early age and he soon showed that he had the makings of an inventor. His enquiring, persistent turn of mind caused him to be fascinated by different types of scientific problem. 'I made hazardous investigations of the principles of flight,' he once recalled, 'launching myself from the tops of haystacks with a home-made hang glider. I almost blew myself up during experiments involving the use of acetylene and water-filled tar barrels – to see how high they could be propelled. In quieter moments I also constructed a primitive electrical recording machine. By such means I learned, the hard way, the fundamentals of reasoning. It was all at the expense of my schooling, where I responded only to the teaching of physics and mathematics with any degree of enthusiasm.'

After leaving school (he attended Magnus Grammar School in Newark) Godfrey had a brief succession of teenage jobs – builder's draughtsman, cinema operator and radio repairman. When war broke out in 1939 he volunteered for the RAF. He became a radar mechanic instructor, having successfully taken an RAF course in radio, and was first posted to the Royal College of Science in South Kensington and then to Cranwell Radar School in Lincolnshire. 'At Cranwell, in my spare time, I sat and passed the City and Guilds examination in radio communications. I also interested myself in constructing demonstration equipment, such as large-scale oscilloscopes, as aids to instruction.'

His work at Cranwell was recognised by the award of a certificate of merit. It was also noticed by a senior RAF officer, an air vice-marshal who ensured that Godfrey obtained a financial grant to pursue his studies once the war had ended.

Leaving the RAF in 1946, Godfrey went to Faraday House College in London where he read electrical and mechanical engineering for four years and gained a diploma. Then, in 1951, at the age of thirty-two, he joined EMI at Hayes in Middlesex. It was the beginning of what was destined to become a truly brilliant career.

In the early 1950s Electrical & Musical Industries Ltd (to give EMI its original name) was engaged in a variety of businesses. First and foremost it was in the recorded music business; but its other activities at that time ranged from the manufacture of gramophones and TV sets to a substantial involvement in defence electronics, notably radar, an involvement stemming from the Second World War. Godfrey's initial work at EMI, in fact, was on radar systems. Before very long, however, he became interested in computers, which were then in their infancy. In 1958, as a project engineer, he headed the EMI team which designed Britain's first large all-transistor computer. This represented a major achievement, for the EMIDEC 1100, as it was called, was technically a highly advanced machine, years ahead of any other computer then on the market. Demand for the 1100 was such that EMI eventually built and sold twenty-four for a total of £6 million.

When he had completed his EMIDEC assignment, Godfrey transferred to EMI's central research laboratories at Hayes and found himself once more involved in computers. He worked for several years on a large-scale computer memory project and then, in 1967, began to explore various aspects of automatic pattern recognition – at that time a purely theoretical science which envisaged computers as being able to recognise and identify images as quickly and efficiently as the human eye and brain.

Arising from his research in this area, Godfrey conceived the idea of harnessing X-rays to computers. This highly innovative concept formed the basis of his subsequent inventions of both brain and whole body scanners. They gave birth to an entirely new branch of medical science – computerised axial tomography, or CAT for short.

By providing, on a linked computer screen, detailed X-ray pictures of 'slices' of the human brain and body, Godfrey's scanner yielded information of a kind never seen before. It was to prove a revolutionary means of medical diagnosis, causing doctors, once they had grasped its full implications, to throw away their text books and start all over again.

However, because it was so revolutionary, Godfrey had considerable difficulty in getting his idea off the ground. The medical profession, extremely conservative in the main, seemingly had little or no confidence in the idea when it was put to them – and in the case of at least one medical professor, no confidence whatever in computers.

Godfrey made contact with officials at the Department of Health and Social Security and talked at length with them. The DHSS appointed a leading bone radiology specialist to review, independently, the entire new scanner concept. His conclusions strongly supported it and the DHSS eventually agreed to offer backing. Godfrey and his two research assistants then constructed a prototype scanner – a crude lash-up affair, built on the bed of an old engineering lathe with bits and pieces of gear gathered from various sources – and made experiments, first with the heads of dead cattle, and later with a preserved section of human brain. The resultant X-ray pictures showed progressively more and more promise as work proceeded over many months. Eventually, in the autumn of 1971, it was felt that the time had come to test the scanner on a living person.

Through the DHSS Godfrey met Dr James Ambrose, a clinical radiologist at Atkinson Morley's Hospital in Wimbledon. The two men took to each other and soon formed a close working relationship. It was arranged that the initial tests on human beings would be undertaken at Atkinson Morley's; and for this purpose an improved prototype was built and installed in the hospital.

The first patient to be scanned was a woman already diagnosed as having tumour of the brain. The scan itself took only a few minutes, but the processing of the resultant X-ray information took many hours. The final pictures, however, convinced Ambrose that they represented a definite breakthrough: the woman had a cystic tumour in her left frontal lobe that could not possibly have been detected unless costly investigative surgery had been undertaken. Ambrose and his medical colleagues were delighted and excited by the scanner's performance.

Further tests on patients resulted in better and better head scans. The time taken to process the resultant pictures was also dramatically improved. The DHSS agreed to purchase the first five machines to be built, for use in British hospitals, and so the stage was set for the news of Godfrey Hounsfield's momentous invention to be broken to the world.

The EMI brain scanner, as the new machine was now called, was publicly launched in April 1972 with a presentation by Godfrey and James Ambrose to an audience of British radiologists. This was followed by a press conference. The radiologists were reported to be flabbergasted. The press, possibly because it could not comprehend the magnitude of Godfrey's invention, took rather longer to respond. A few months later, in the summer of 1972, Godfrey whetted the appetites of radiologists in New York. Together with Dr James Bull, a leading London neurologist, he presented a series of lectures there on CAT scanning. Then, in November 1972, came the annual convention in Chicago of the Radiological Society of North America. Attended by 2,000 doctors and radiologists from all over the USA and Canada, and also from various other parts of the world, the excitement generated when James Ambrose showed the results of the clinical trials knew no bounds. Hospitals and medical clinics throughout North America, as well as in Japan, Germany and other countries, started to clamour for EMI brain scanners. They all wanted them, and as soon as possible.

No doubt because profits from the new scanner invention had yet to show in EMI's balance sheet, City awareness of the importance of what was happening was still not strongly apparent. In the medical world, however, the soaring excitement in North America literally travelled back to Britain across the Atlantic. Increasing numbers of doctors and radiologists flew in to Heathrow from the

States, to inspect personally one of the few EMI scanners then available at Hayes. Initial production of the machines was slow; delivery times of six months or so were being quoted, but this in no way deterred prospective customers.

Godfrey himself, meanwhile, was rightly beginning to be recognised by the outside world for his great achievement. The first of what was to become a lengthy list of honours and distinctions over the next few years was made in 1972, when his invention won for EMI and himself the MacRobert Award consisting of £25,000 and a gold medal. He received it, as he did all subsequent awards made to him, with his customary modesty. A diffident bachelor of frugal habits, he seemed largely uninterested in personal possessions, his mind constantly immersed in the complexities of his work.

The scanner continued to climb from one level of success to another. Orders flowed in from hospitals and clinics all over the world, as well as from North America, and a fast-moving medical business – an entirely new business for EMI – was beginning to make a substantial contribution to profits. In 1974 Godfrey, whose ever-restless mind and researches had been exploring further possibilities, announced that whole-body scanning was feasible. A prototype machine was accordingly made to undertake tests and in 1975, at an international symposium of radiologists in Bermuda, Godfrey showed the first results. They consisted of 'slices' of his own body obtained by scans made under laboratory conditions at Hayes. The audience burst into spontaneous applause, although Godfrey himself was as modest as ever when he showed them.

The year 1975 marked a high point in the CAT scanner story. The news of Godfrey's latest invention spread like wildfire through the international medical profession. In London *The Times* ran a front-page story emphasising the importance of Godfrey's work. The international media immediately followed this up, and over the ensuing weeks a flood of press, radio and TV enquiries ensued. The City and Wall Street got excited too, with investment analysts and brokers scenting ever-greater profits to be made, so that EMI shares became, (temporarily, at least) the hottest property in the financial markets. One Wall Street analyst flew in specially to Hayes, spent thirty minutes looking at the prototype body scanner and asking one or two questions, then flew back to New York to recommend a strong 'buy' of EMI stock.

Soon after Godfrey's sensational demonstration at Bermuda, moves to step up production of both types of EMI scanner got under way. In Britain, output at Hayes was supplemented by the opening of a new factory at Aldenham. Overseas, because the United States had always been rightly perceived as the world's wealthiest and most responsive medical market, plans to establish a factory for EMI scanner production, on a site just outside Chicago, were also put in hand.

It was at this point, however, around the middle of 1976, that the bandwagon began to hit commercial and political problems. Although orders continued to roll in to EMI for both types of scanner, competitors were beginning to emerge. Despite the worldwide patenting of Godfrey's invention, foreign companies in the medical electronics field were in no way deterred from launching scanners of their own – having by now got to grips with the new technology.

Even more ominously, following President Carter's election in 1977, the United States Government decided to embark on a programme of health-care cost containment under which expensive body scanners, however effective, became the prime target. Orders in the US started to decline sharply as a result. Elsewhere in the world, notably in Japan, the UK and mainland Europe, orders were still being well maintained but could not match the volume being lost in the USA.

EMI was also beginning to experience difficulties in other directions. Its music operations ran into a sudden downturn – the victim of a major recession in the recorded music business worldwide. Combined with the deteriorating EMI-Scanner situation, where mounting costs in the USA were also seriously affecting profitability (the Chicago factory never really got going), EMI as a company suffered a double blow from which it did not recover. Within three years, by 1980, it had been forced to withdraw completely from medical electronics operations and to sell its Scanner interests to competitors.

The extraordinary abruptness of EMI's departure from the world medical scene nevertheless could not detract from its earlier achievements in successfully launching CAT scanners on the market – let alone from the pioneering achievements of Godfrey Hounsfield himself. Over a period of five years, from 1972 to 1977, EMI sold just over 700 brain and body Scanners to hospital and clinics in thirty countries – the majority, 460, to the United States.

Godfrey, in the meantime, became rightly famed and honoured. He was made a Fellow of the Royal Society in 1975, appointed CBE in 1976 and knighted in 1981. Academic honours were showered upon him: between 1972 and 1980 he was the recipient of six honorary degrees from universities and more than forty prestigious awards by scientific institutions throughout the world.

In 1979 he also became a Nobel Prize winner. He shared the award with an American physicist, Allan Macleod Cormack, who had pursued independent research into the theory of computerised tomography at Tufts University in the mid-1960s. Godfrey was completely unaware of Cormack's work in the same field, as the Nobel authorities officially acknowledged. The two men received the prize for 'the development of computer-assisted tomography'. Godfrey's own work was described in the Nobel citation as 'epoch-making in medical radiology... with an unusual combination of vision, intuition and imagination, and with an extraordinarily sure eye for the optimal choice of physical factors in a system that must have offered very great problems to construct, he obtained results which in one blow surprised the medical world. It can be no exaggeration to maintain that no other method within X-ray diagnostics has, during such a short period of time, led to such remarkable advances.'

The news of Godfrey's Nobel award first reached EMI in a rather surprising fashion. I was sitting in my office late one October morning in 1979 when the phone rang and a man on the Associated Press news desk in New York spoke to me. He said that the AP office in Stockholm had heard unofficially that Godfrey Hounsfield was the joint winner of a Nobel Prize: could I confirm it? I said I couldn't. I did not think that anyone in EMI knew anything about it, and rang off. Immediately afterwards I quickly organised some enquiries within the company and it appeared that indeed we did not know anything about it. However, after representations to Stockholm, the Nobel Foundation put out a statement later that day confirming that the 1979 Nobel Prize for Physiology or Medicine (to give the formal title) had been jointly awarded to Allan Cormack and Godfrey.

With the official breaking of the news we had to move fast, as always in the news-handling business. Press enquiries started to flow in during the afternoon and Godfrey had to be contacted – to ask if he would be prepared to give an immediate press conference. He agreed, and within an hour or so we had science correspondents from national newspapers, news agency reporters, overseas correspondents based in London, and a complete CBS TV crew who wanted the story for New York – all assembled in a Central London hotel. Godfrey himself, when he appeared, was as relaxed and courteous as ever, but obviously a little tired. He answered all questions put to him with great patience, explaining to the uninitiated how a CAT scanner worked and, in more personal terms, what he would do with his share of the Nobel Prize money. ('I shall equip a room in my house,' he modestly told a *Daily Express* reporter, 'and potter about with interesting ideas. It's my hobby.')

I have a final recollection of Godfrey at the conference. I was listening to him talking to a *Daily Telegraph* correspondent about the hundreds of letters he received from people all over the world whose illnesses had been successfully diagnosed as a result of his scanner inventions. 'I get regular letters from patients,' he said. 'It's one of the greatest bonuses of my work.'

(From *Personal Encounters* by Bryan Samain.
Pentland Press, 2000.)